W9-BCS-414

Riding the Tiger

RIDING THE TIGER

Ramiro de León Carpio's Battle For Human Rights in Guatemala

ALVARO VARGAS LLOSA
AND
SANTIAGO AROCA

Brickell Communications
Miami, Florida

Translated from an unpublished transcript by Carlos Verdecia

Library of Congress Catalog Card Number: 95-80188

ISBN 0-9648426-0-2

PRINTED IN THE UNITED STATES OF AMERICA

"It is useless to maintain that social progress takes place by itself, bit by bit, in virtue of the spiritual conditions of the society at a certain period of its history. It is really a leap forward which is only taken when the society has made up its mind to try an experiment; this means that the society must have allowed itself to be convinced, or at any rate allowed itself to be shaken; and the shake is always given by somebody."

H. Bergson

Contents

Prologue

As our helicopter rose over the Guatemalan plateau and our eyes filled with undulating volcanos, lakes and depths, the voice of President Ramiro de León Carpio, less than a foot away, faded into a distant rumor. We were traveling to Escuintla, near the Pacific Ocean, to visit Santo Tomás ranch, the 100-acre retreat the infamous Gen. Jorge Ubico built half a century ago to accommodate a universe of deer, lizard woods, polygons, army barracks and sports arenas. Miguel Angel Asturias's words about Escuintla came to mind — he called it the "poinsettia flower at America's waistline" — and I thought of all the providential accidents that killed political experiments in similar aircrafts. In the facial expressions of the pilot and captain who escorted us I tried to detect some indication that either my brains were shortly to spatter the majestic volcano caressing the chopper's belly, or that we would soon be splashing into the immemorial waters of the taciturn lake.

It was in this paradise resort that my lengthy conversation with President De León Carpio took place. The dialogue, which gave flesh to this book, searched into the personal, intellectual and political intimacies of this former Human Rights Commissioner risen to power by sheer fate.

Ramiro de León Carpio's figure is, in various ways, atypical in Latin America. Here is a man coming from the shore opposite the apparatus of power in a country where the dominant caste — civilian and military — and the guerrilla insurrection have for many years delayed Guatemala's entrance to modernness. Leaning on the symbolism of having reached the presidency after President Jorge Serrano Elías's coup attempt failed, and after having established — albeit over obstacles and setbacks — the basis for incorporating the guerrillas to civilian life, this man, a believer in notions as far-fetched as legality, institutional continuity and peace, has managed to preserve the democratic system. How can anyone be a human rights champion and at the same time lead a country that for so long has antagonized such a philosophy? What is the political and personal price that must be paid to survive inside institutions so deeply marked by the imprint of violence and corruption, the very habits to be reformed?

From our altitude, nature's muted peace sharply contrasted with the deafening saber-rattling noise that has overwhelmed the history of Guatemala, a country where a false conflict between liberals and conservatives wasted its republican life throughout a succession of dictatorships that did not subside even under the great "liberal" reform of 1871.

The 20th Century saw no improvement. Another parade of despots marched through power until the 1944 revolution, when Juan José Arévalo, sensing the need of a political shakeup — just as Jacobo Arbenz did later — eagerly pursued the mistaken idea that confiscation and collectivism were a valid strategy to battle the privileges of the United Fruit Co. and the big plantation owners, as if wealth were but an equation adding up to zero. From then on, while the world engaged in reaching up to the moon and down to the privacy of the atom, Guatemala used its imagination to induct and remove dictators upheld or opposed by a mafia of powerful interests that treated political power like a collection agency.

A bunch of petty men, no less astray than the others, began a long, still ongoing, epic era of blood and fire, dressed in the ideological color in vogue and nurtured by Cuba and other power centers. They successfully served the purpose of delivering Guatemala's destiny to the military, whose vertical vision of society, patrimonial concept of government, and violent methodology ended up alienating any possibility of a law-driven peaceful world, one in which freedom wouldn't be under suspicion. False dialectics between the guerrillas and the military obscured the only decent option. And today this President who sat at my side gravitated toward an alternative — a negotiated peace — which, while debatable, seemed politically inevitable.

From a helicopter, Guatemala looks uniform. It isn't. It's rather a world of cultural traumas with no solution yet to the big issue: the cohabitation of cultures crossing through diverse historical stages. Although Professor Armando de la Torre believes, with optimism, that one percent of the indigenous people is assimilated by the Ladino culture every year, perhaps a little more caution may be advisable. Are the atavisms of three million Indians compatible with modern ways? Is there anything in common between the Gutierrezes, who have inundated Central America with "Campero Chicken," and the Quiché Indians to whom primitive barter transactions and the agriculture of subsistence still make sense? While the copter's propeller deafened us, it was hard to remain lucid enough to reflect on the tension between the ethical ideal — the Indians' pace — and the ideal of "progress," under which Indians would be circumstantially assimilated into the Ladino culture and their customs reduced to a ritual symbolism. The gray area would imply that Popol Vuh's milpa and the cult of Tecún Umán, the Quiché leader who fell in combat against the Spaniards while his pet (a beautiful quetzal) took flight into the skies, will not stand in the way of the Quiché Indians into modernness.

Ironic. The guerrillas have tried to settle over indigenous roots not realizing that their communication with the past is just as blocked, and their ideological petrification, their warfare strategy, their passion for publicity, and their intellectualization of Indian issues as foreign to the Indian as their own enemies — the military and the bureaucrats. Modernness has been a crossfire of bullets and unintelligible words.

Mythology has hurt cultural thinking in Guatemala. For starters, there is no unique "indigenous world." The incommunication between Quiché, Kakchikel and Kekchi Indians, to mention only three of more than twenty ethnic groups, is abysmal, and the relations between the first two are harsh, since the Kakchikels of the Atitlán Lake collaborated with the Spaniards against the Quiché Indians. The peaceful Kekchis who guard the entrance to Petén Lake are more advanced than the Quiché Indians of remote San Marcos. It would be inaccurate to affirm that all Indians live in a world dating back to an era prior of trading. Their artisanal craft for export and their commercial instinct delineate their modern face, which like Janus's has its counterpart: the agriculture of subsistence, by which half-a-million agricultural estates are ruled by ancestral customs, broken into mini-estates to be parceled out by their children, and atomized at a pace opposite to that of a scale economy, which forces peasant children to work as laborers in the coffee harvest. Yet the fact that many joined in civil self-defense patrols against the guerrillas and feel appreciation for their property is perhaps an indication that they are not so different.

When we flew over the Palín Canyon between the Water Volcano and the Fire Volcano, the peaceful landscape suggested patience and a belief that these enigmas will resolve by themselves, that culture is a substance made of time, and that what's done intentionally will turn harmful, if only because no mind is capable of predicting the pace at which human culture can change or wishes to change, nor which elements will prompt a transformation with the least of traumas. The government's obligation, of course, is not to distribute land based on "cultural seniority," nor prevent the Indians from owning the land.

Only 10 percent of the Guatemalan economy is state-run, and the government consumes barely 6 percent of the national product. Not enough. In addition to generating three decades of violence, politicians, bureaucrats and the military have done little more than waste time. Powerful businessmen have blackmailed the government (and the government has permitted it) into thwarting healthy competition, in the same manner that now labor unions want to prevent mediocre public services from being better managed by civil society. Decisions have hinged on corruption, and property rights have gotten less respect that human life. The way power is exercised in Guatemala constitutes the primary source of its pain.

Without realizing it, we landed and were at the entrance of Santo Tomás. A man saluted and, from the bottom of Latin American history — perhaps not understanding why, moved more by a subordination instinct than by an aware sense of government and its laws — he pronounced a loud "Mr. President." Our conversation was about to begin.

Alvaro Vargas Llosa
London, June 1995

1

The Rigors of Childhood

Question*: President De León Carpio, you were born in 1942. What do you remember of the Guatemala of your childhood? Where did you live the first years of your life?*

Ramiro de León Carpio: Mine was a very *sui generis* birth. When I became old enough to understand I was told that my father was not at my mother's side the day of my birth. My father, José Martín De León Muñoz, had gone to fight in World War II. The day of my birth my father was on military duty in the Philippines as a member of the United States Army. I did not meet him until after the war.

Q: *Who replaced your father at home?*

RDLC: My maternal grandmother replaced my father. My mother too, but my maternal grandmother, who had a very strong character, headed the household and had great influence on me as the youngest child. She came from a very powerful Guatemalan family linked to national politics. My grandmother was an orphan at age 15 with seven siblings.

First she lost her mother and then her father. As a child she was called to assume great responsibilities. She was a well read woman, reading anything she could get her hands on. She devoured books and magazines like the Reader's Digest. She also was an avid reader of news, always looking out for newspapers. Even when she was over 90 years old, she continued to be a woman of great character. Indeed, she replaced my father on many occasions. Not only when my father was absent during the war, but on other occasions as well.

My father was a very special man. He belonged to a very wealthy agricultural elite and had a lot of money, which made him a man of the world. He took every opportunity to travel. It's true that he had this bohemian streak and he could enjoy life anywhere. My father lived and went to school in Paris, and later moved to San Francisco, California. He led a very diverse and cosmopolitan life, which often forced him to be absent from home. During a great part of my life my maternal grandmother took my father's place. It was she who educated me and my siblings. Especially me because I always lived very close to her.

My grandmother and my mother had a very special way of complementing each other and communicating. My mother is a woman of extreme and profound goodness, part of which we inherited. A very special humanitarian sensitivity which my grandmother also had, but she had a stronger personality. The important decisions in the family were left to my grandmother. My mother was a little fearful when faced with the big things in life, whereas my grandmother always displayed plenty of character, courage and boldness. My grandmother's name was Mercedes de la Cerda Alejos de Carpio, a woman with a stern personality, very Catholic, and with a broad social sensitivity.

Q: *Do you feel resentment for your father's absence during your early years?*

RDLC: I'm not exactly resentful, but it did have an impact on me. A permanent sense of lacking. Other kids had their father; I didn't. One of my older brothers reproached my father a lot for this.

My father left home for the war at the end of 1941. I was born in January of 1942. My father returned in 1945 or 1946, I don't remember exactly when. And he didn't stay for long. His second absence marked another stage of my life. We were no longer living in Guatemala, but in the south of Mexico, in Chiapas. Because of my father's absence and our financial problems we moved to Mexico, where my grandmother had relatives. There I studied my first years of grammar school. Not only did I learn Mexican history before the Guatemalan, but I also memorized the Mexican national anthem before the Guatemalan anthem. My first news about Guatemala when I started to gain conscience were about prior dictators — Manuel Estrada Cabrera, who remained in power 22 years, and Gen. Jorge Ubico, who ruled for 14 years. The Guatemala of my first memories was a world of convulsion full of oppression.

Q: *Did you and your family keep a permanent contact with Guatemala from Mexico, or was it lost?*

RDLC: We never lost contact. We had relatives in Guatemala who visited us constantly. The concept of geographical border was very blurry. Mexico City is very far from Chiapas and during those first years of adolescence it was not very clear we were in another country. For a long time it seemed we were still in Guatemala.

Besides, some in our family were involved in politics. They told us about things. We did not learn through the radio, for instance, that Col. Jacobo Arbenz would assume power after Dr. Juan José Arévalo. We learned about it through comments within the family. When it finally happened, it seemed normal. "Sure, it's Arbenz. Just like your uncle said," my grandmother said.

Q: *Chiapas is a mountainous region with much misery, very poor, where lies a problem shared by Guatemala. We are referring to the cohabitation of diverse cultures — the indigenous and the westernized world. These are cultures that live in very different histori-*

cal times. Tell us about your first contact with the indigenous world. What do you remember? When was the first time you saw an Indian?

RDLC: Our life transpired principally in the city of Tapachula. But when my father returned from the war, he decided to again devote his efforts to agriculture and he bought a farm in Cacahuatán, which in 1994-95 became one of the centers of the insurrection by the Zapatista Army of National Liberation. My father's farm was located in what would later become Zapatista territory.

It was in that farm where I had my first meaningful contact with the indigenous people. What I remember most is a Chamula Indian, of the Chamula tribes, who lived in terrible poverty. I can still picture clearly in my memory watching the Indian hanging rats from a wire. He skinned them and then ate them. These people lived in absolute misery, almost in Stone Age conditions. Society denied them everything. I remember those Indians — and I have thought about them a thousand times because they are lasting images of my childhood — as victims of tremendous injustices. Poverty, misery. That's the memory I keep of my first contact with the indigenous world. Recently I found a photograph of those years in which I am riding a horse accompanied by farm servants, and these boys are wearing extremely poor clothes, showing an extraordinary level of poverty.

We're talking about Mexico, but Guatemala was just as bad. The indigenous population suffered the same unrelenting poverty, the same abandonment, enduring indescribable abuse.

Q: *Do you remember any contact with indigenous groups in Guatemala before moving to Mexico?*

RDLC: Not before I went to Mexico because I was very little. Later I did.

Q: *How did your mother and grandmother relate to indigenous persons? How did your family see the Indians?*

RDLC: They had an attitude of compassion, of solidarity. The three heads of the family — my father, my mother and my grandmother — represented three different attitudes very common in our world. My father, who came from a wealthy family and had been a millionaire in his childhood although he later became penniless, expressed certain social sensitivity toward them. I imagine he acquired it in time because I doubt that he would have had that same attitude as an 8-year-old living in opulence.

My grandmother, who was not a millionaire but came from a powerful and well-to-do family that placed her in a very special environment of the Guatemalan high society, was very cordial and understanding toward the Indians. She used to say life had sensitized her.

My mother was born tender and sensitive. All three ended up feeling sympathy toward the suffering of others. All three, with their differences, taught us to be humble before that reality. In the case of my grandmother, with a harsher character but always with great humanity.

For those reasons, no one in my house had any misgivings about my playing with indigenous children or relating to them. In my house all those present when my grandmother served dinner sat at the table. There was no ethnic distinction whatsoever.

Q: *In the Guatemala of the 40s and 50s many important events took place. In the Guatemala of the 50s there was a movement that ended up with a military intervention to topple President Arbenz. How do you remember the era of Presidents Arévalo and Arbenz?*

RDLC: The years of President Arévalo were those of an excellent statesman. Arévalo was a great humanist with an exceptional sense of progress for mankind. However, at the advent of President Arbenz to power, the news I heard through my family, owner of vast farmlands, was that Arbenz was a communist. With Arbenz my house burst with rumors and excitement. To some he was a big threat. Other spoke of him in terms of hope. I suppose there was truth on both sides.

Early I heard that with Arbenz came the agrarian reform, the tortures. The notorious police chiefs were discussed with fear. My grandmother used to lower her voice to pronounce their names. I still remember one of them as Rosemberg and the other one a Cruz Wer. The mere mention of them was believed to be an omen of an evil occurrence.

These are the things I remember. Some true; other exaggerated. In any case, I perceived the arrival of Arbenz as a threat. At that time we had returned to Guatemala after our house in Tapachula, Chiapas, was destroyed by fire. It was something terrible beyond our control. The fire started in a neighboring hardware store. I was seven or eight. I remember I was playing in the house when the noise lured me to the street. I saw these huge flames coming out of this hardware store whose name I will never forget: Casa Henkel. With the flames came huge explosions of big cans of paint and chemicals. Actually, the fire itself did not reach my house, but the firemen and looters destroyed it alleging they did it to prevent the flames from expanding.

The fire revealed many things, among them what everyone owned at that moment. When I stepped out to watch the fire I was hypnotized by the huge flames, probably 60 to 70 feet high. My brother, however, who had played in the local soccer team, ran inside the house and challenged the flames to recover his soccer ball and boots. Another brother — the eldest, the exemplary student destined to be an engineer— took out his books. While everyone saved what each treasured most I went into total anguish to help people. When I came out of my shock I made sure my mother, my grandmother and my younger brother had left the house. Worrying about others I did not save anything special of my belongings. I later regretted failing to save some toys I treasured dearly.

We lost everything. All of a sudden we were surrounded by ashes. For this reason my grandmother, my father and my mother decided to move back to Guatemala. Had it not been for the fire, I never would have become president of Guatemala.

Q: *The fire changed your life then, but what happened to your family? Did they all return to Guatemala?*

RDLC: Not everyone. The family was divided again and my grandmother and one of my brothers, the eldest, remained in Mexico so that he could finish secondary school. I was in grammar school and my mother decided to bring the rest of us back to Guatemala and managed to make my father stay with us. We did not move to the capital city, though. We went to Escuintla, to a place named Cerritos. There my father established a citronella plantation with a very creative partner named Mynor Kilahuer. Cerritos was not only agricultural; it also had a paper plant. We used to sell citronella to produce paper and to extract oil from it.
Q: *When you arrived in Guatemala, didn't you fear that the agrarian reform would affect you and eventually seize your land?*
RDLC: No, because the reform only affected unused land. My father stayed behind in the farm while we went to the city of Escuintla to study. There is something I remember vividly. Every Saturday I would come out with some of my friends to watch Col. Arbenz pass by with his escort on his way to his nearby farm named El Cajón. We greeted him without exactly knowing what his government represented.

That ended when the entire family returned to Guatemala City to live together. During that time there were events that left an imprint on me for the rest of my life. It was 1953 and I started at a Jesuit school, Liceo Javier, to study my fourth grade. Religious education, combined with the Catholic formation I had received at home, made a serious impact in my life. And in 1954 Arbenz was overthrown.

My perception of those events was very much like the majority of the people. Were we facing an invasion, or was our country being saved? I would later realize, like the rest of the country, that it was an invasion promoted by the U.S. Central Intelligence Agency to protect, among other things, the interests of American companies. This is a well-known fact today. You only need to read the book "Bitter Fruit" (*Fruta Amarga*) written by two American journalists.
Q: *You were very young, but what do you remember of the political climate prior to the invasion? Were there secret contacts? Did you*

experience conspiratory anti-government activity within your house?
RDLC: Of course, my family always housed a broad variety of political shades and some of our close relatives took part in the invasion. They truly believed it was the salvation of the country.
Q: *Do you still believe that, as was said at the moment, the reforms President Arbenz promoted actually moved the country close to communism? Or is that, viewed under contemporary eyes, a mere exaggeration?*
RDLC: With time I have of course formed my own opinion. I believe that the program of the Arbenz Administration was terrific and simply nationalistic. It presented three fundamental parts that had nothing to do with communism: one aimed at boosting energy production through the Jurum Marinalá project to compete with Bond Shire and Co., the American company that had a monopoly. Viewed under today's light, Jurum Marinalá, which still generates some 60 megawatts, made a lot of sense. A second part was the Atlantic highway, the most important road today connecting the Atlantic and the Pacific Oceans, but viewed then as a threat to the International Railroads of Central America, a railroad company owned by American capital. The highway took away passengers and cargo from rail transportation, another foreign-owned monopoly. The third element was the agrarian reform, the famous Decree 900, whose purpose was to eliminate unused land. If we compare this law with other laws and land transformations we have had afterward, it was nothing out of this world. But it affected another American interest, the United Fruit Co. Compared to the Salvadoran land reform carried out in the 90s, the Arbenz version was minuscule.

The fundamental issue was where Arbenz was headed. With great charisma and control over the people, President Arbenz was called the "Soldier of the People." He was a man of great social sensitivity surrounded by the very people who later started the communist organizations that have challenged the Guatemalan government in the last decades. From Arbenz's entourage came, for example, the Guatemalan Labor Party (PGT) which gave base to the guerrillas.

I now insist that Arbenz was a great man, a great soldier, a very nationalistic person with a great sense of honesty.

Q: *Is it possible then to say that Arbenz created the conditions for the birth of the guerrillas?*

RDLC: In a certain way, yes. The Communist Party and the principal communist leaders the country has had derived from Arbenz's government. What I have never been able to verify is whether Arbenz himself was totally convinced. I have the impression that no, that he never knew he was surrounded by communist advisors. He was a good, nationalistic officer who loved his country.

His first big mistake was to confront the American economic interests so radically, knowing that the first land-tenant in the country was the United Fruit Co. The truth is that in all its other points his program worked. The energy sector in Guatemala was open to competition, and the highway linking the Atlantic and the Pacific is still used.

Another negative element in the Arbenz Administration was the country's polarization and acting against the anticommunists. It fractured the nation in a way that has not healed yet, despite the years and the fact that communism has disappeared as a political alternative.

Q: *Perhaps an important factor was the different light under which foreign capital was seen. As of the decade of the 80s, all foreign countries competed to invest, but it was not so before. Foreign capital was equated to political oppression, to imperialism. How did you perceive the presence of foreign capital in those years of the 50s and the 60s?*

RDLC: During that time, and long after, any foreign investment prompted the idea that its purpose was to steal our resources. Not only in agriculture, but also with minerals. Today you find the opposite is true. At that moment, there was a big campaign against the transnationals, which were then called multinationals and were depicted as a great octopus capable of eating everything up.

Q: *How did the farmers and industrialists perceive the participation of American capital in Guatemala in the 60s?*

RDLC: Globally, I would say that positively. Investments generated jobs. It was also good from the productivity standpoint. What they resented was not being allowed to compete, like they are able to do now. In those years you could not plant bananas without authorization from United Fruit, and much less generate energy. It was a monopoly regime protected by whoever had his turn in the palace. Transportation, bananas and energy were monopolies. This was not well seen, but then there was the alleged threat of communism. This is the reason the entrepreneurs got involved in the invasion that toppled Arbenz. And it wasn't only the invasion, backed by the CIA and the American ambassador, but also the uprising in the interior of the country.

Q: *What do you remember of the invasion?*

RDLC: Many moments that were ever so important. My family lived then in a centric zone of Guatemala City, where there was a nearby airport. The day the invasion began we heard many airplanes taking off. We kids called this operation "*sulfato*", a sulfate-based medication used in Guatemala to treat constipation. We used to joke that the planes would lighten the bowels of those defending the regime.

I also remember how we hid in the dark to listen to the news on a clandestine radio station because in the climate of terror Arbenz had created one never knew if a neighbor would denounce you. But I remember listening when the army surrendered and it was announced that Arbenz was fleeing the country to exile, where he died. It seemed sad. Particularly the way he was humiliated and all his properties confiscated, most of which he had owned before he had assumed power. It was shocking that even his wife's jewelry was expropriated, and it wasn't until 1994 when I, as president, returned this jewelry, which had been locked up in a safety box in the Central Bank of Guatemala. I gave them to Arbenz's widow, who lived in Costa Rica with her children and grandchildren.

In those days of the coup and the invasion there was hardly any time for reflection. I remember two of my cousins showed up at my family's house in uniform after participating in the invasion. One of them was Roberto Carpio, who would later become the nation's vice president.

Q: *In the wake of the invasion, Guatemalan politics turned somewhat unstable, very uncertain. How did this instability affect you?*

RDLC: A lot. It changed my family life. My family was very interested in politics. My grandmother would comment on everything. Family and politics have marked my life. The first five-year period of my life transpired under a dictatorship. During the second there was the fire in Mexico, the return to the upheaval prompted by the advent of President Arbenz, and the Jesuit school. And my third five-year period was marked by yet another political change: The toppling of Arbenz and the rise to power of Carlos Castillo Armas. In the following five-year period — and this was already 1956 — the assassination of Castillo Armas was important. Besides, the Jesuits expelled me from their school.

Q: *Why were you expelled?*

RDLC: For rebellion. For challenging. For being a leader. Not because I was a bad student; I always got good grades. I will never forget that the priest who expelled me told my mother and my grandmother (my father was half absent and it was my grandmother who always discussed things with the school principal) that he expelled me because I was a leader. My grandmother replied, "Well, if you kick him out because he is dangerous, you will regret it." She advised them to allow me to stay to straighten out, but they wouldn't.

Q: *But was there a special reason for expelling you?*

RDLC: Of course they had a formal motive. A spiritual retreat was the straw on the camel back. I had been warned. There were two activities going on — one was soccer, which was always present in my life. We had organized a school team to play against other schools in a tournament. But the Jesuits would not let us go to the game. Then I organized an escape and we went to our game. When we returned the following day we got expelled and I was readmitted under one condition: one more admonition and I would never be allowed to return to school. That second reprimand occurred when there was a spiritual retreat in the city of Antigua and some disorder took place, probably caused by our young age. I was only 15. We escaped from the retreat at night and things got complicated because of the harsh discipline of the Jesuits. We were taken out of the retreat and sent back to Guatemala. When we arrived at the school we were expelled. I and others as well.

This was an important development. First, I was not able to graduate from the school Liceo Javier. This caused great concerns in the family. It was a big blow to my grandmother. I registered in another school, where things worked out well and I graduated. I continued my education and moved on, and soon it was all forgotten. My grandmother did not reproach me anymore.

Q: *In the 60s university life came to you. You went to the National University of San Carlos, the only one in the country before the Jesuits opened their own Catholic university. Did you not?*

RDLC: Here again, with political and family activities running parallel, this decade represented the start of another five-year period. From 1960 to 1965 I decided to register at the National University. The expulsion from the Jesuit school had forced me to take a broader look at reality and I had taken up classes with someone who exerted a strong influence on me — Severo Martínez, author of *La Patria del Criollo*. He was a historian, a sociologist with Marxist ideas, as well as a man of high intellect.

I don't keep bad memories of the Jesuit teachings. I liked the fact that they taught things as they really were. This is good. I liked it so much that my children went to their school, and I later graduated with them. Various things had happened and I had finished my secondary education at age 18.

At that time I participated in speech contests at school and competed with some characters who today are public figures. I also did some stage acting. All in spite of being a shy kid. I overcame my own shyness because I enjoyed doing these things. I came out on the stage and faced the audience. On Mother's Day I would read a poem, and I particularly liked one that said, "There are no more orphans." It made the ladies cry. I remember the poem said there were no more orphans because, despite losing their mothers, children always had the Virgin Mary. I did not know then how much that meant to a father or a grandmother caring for an orphan child. In the theater I once played the part of San Ignacio de Loyola in a group with other characters who ended up in public life. *El Divino Impaciente* was the name of the play. Despite being shy, my life always gravitated to the public arena because of my leadership traits.

In 1960 I registered at the National University of San Carlos and passed the first year. During those five years at the university two important events took place. The first one, I started dating the person who later became my wife and the mother of my children, Mayra Duque Valenzuela.

Q: *Was she your first girlfriend?*

RDLC: Not really. I had other girlfriends before, but Mayra was the first I took seriously and the first one I married. I met her in 1962 and we married in January of 1966.

The university made a significant political impact on me. In those years the guerrilla penetration in the university was very strong. Many of my classmates would later become members and commanders of the guerrilla. One of them, César Macías, whose war name was César Montes, became famous and is now retired in El Salvador. I arrived at the university eager to be active. The first thing I did was take part in the elections for the student board of directors supporting Hugo Argueta against the Christian Democrats, who made their first appearance in national politics. It was there, at the San Carlos university where I gave my first public speech.

Q: *Which side did you take in a university fragmented among Christian Democrats and guerrilla supporters?*

RDLC: Because of my marked sensitivity for social issues I gravitated toward the left, although I also had good friends on the right. My inclination toward the left, however, made me break up with them. Perhaps the logical thing would have been to approach the Christian Democrat movement that emerged with a center-to-right position.

At that moment my family inclined to the right, although my immediate family — my mother and my grandmother — tilted to the left. My father, always half-absent, hardly mattered. I was plugged to reality, to the misery I had known in Mexico. Besides, I had a Christian social formation and developed a sense toward humanitarian issues. In those days the phrase human rights was hardly used. The terms humanitarian sensitivity, social sensitivity were more broadly used.

I also had to live through the end of my family's economic peak. My older siblings knew what abundance was like. I didn't. We didn't go to Chiapas as tourists. We went there to work. It doesn't mean I am resentful. I never was, but I always cared about other people's hardships.

I came very close to Marxism, but my grandmother rescued me. She knew who my friends were and overheard many of our conversations. Her serious concerns about where I was heading prompted her to seek a scholarship that would get me out and through international law school. She finally got it in 1962 through her many influential friends.

I had serious doubts that violence was the way. Fortunately, I was immunized against the guerilla. I can't stand violence, I do not tolerate injustice, and I love freedom. Those are the three principles that have led my life. To such extent that now that I am on a diet it bothers me not being able to eat anything I want. I have always acted openly provided I did not upset anyone.

All these thoughts helped me accept my grandmother's advice and I left with the scholarship. First, I went to Mexico. I was supposed to go to school and stay with my grandmother's brothers, but that alternative didn't work out and I had to come home. My grandmother then obtained financial help and sent me to Spain, where I stayed only a few months. Back in Guatemala I started working in the daily *El Gráfico* with my brother Carlos Enrique. I also began managing a relative's business that took me to Honduras. Nostalgia made me return after it became very clear that I wanted to marry Mayra. Before the wedding, however, I registered in the university. I had learned that a new Jesuit university, the Rafael Landivar Catholic University, had opened. I registered there after San Carlos university's program changed to require all its students to have a general formation in science and letters. The idea was to finish quickly and get married, although I ended up alternating work and studies after I finally decided to marry before graduating. After the required six years, I received my law and notary degree.

Q: *Why did you study law?*

RDLC: I had a natural inclination toward law, to litigation, debate. Social science always appealed to me and it was in this area where I mostly excelled. Besides, I had this tendency to always help. An attorney has two options: to become rich defending big economic interests such as the powerful enterprises; or to help others. I know many great lawyers who could have made huge fortunes but opted for the second choice. Others were even murdered for doing just that. Alfonso Bauer Paiz, the refugees' attorney, to name one. He had been a cabinet member and friend of Arbenz, and when he went into exile he became the attorney of the poorest. While that was not exactly my goal, my inclination moved in that direction.

It was in those years when I read Marx, Engels, Camilo Torres, Che Guevara and Mario Palleras, the Guatemalan who wrote "The Days of the Jungle" *(Los Días de la Jungla).* Something stopped me, however. I agreed with the concept of denouncing injustice to eventually change society, but I disagreed on the methods. Present circumstances serve to confirm that I was right.

Indians and Ladinos

By Santiago Aroca

Half of Guatemala's 9.7 million population are considered Ladinos, a mixture of European and Indian blood. The other half are pure Indians who, according to a 1995 United Nations human rights report, "remain largely outside the country's political, social and economic mainstream." The U.N. report indicates that Guatemala's illiteracy is as high as 52 percent and that only 29 percent of the Indian population can read and write.

Despite its small size, Guatemala's Indian population is fragmented for historical and cultural reasons. Among other manifestations of such division, the Indians speak 23 different dialects.

The incorporation of the Indian population in Guatemala has always been a problem. During the Spanish rule, for example, King Charles III was outraged to hear about the huge massacres with which his soldiers quelled the Mayan rebellions in 1760 and 1764. The King was so impressed by what he heard that he sent a special envoy to verify the conditions under which Indians worked in the large plantations of sugar cane and indigo.

The envoy, Archbishop Pedro Cortés y Larrazábal, could only learn that the Indians did not want to be subjected to slavery. "These damned beings absolutely loathe Spaniards," he wrote the court. The Archbishop's report is but one of the many compiled in 300 years of Spanish rule during which there were more than 30 indigenous rebellions.

In this century, the wars carried on by the Indians have caused more than 100,000 victims. In Guatemala, the conflict was not one between the CIA and Karl Marx's disciples, but a clash of two societies — Indians and Ladinos — from the very beginning of colonization.

The cross and the sword have been replaced by more modern ways of annihilation, but the vectors that have guided history remain unaltered. Indians deprived of lands occupy plantations owned by the rich, who in turn pay police to evict them, as President Ramiro de León Carpio has denounced repeatedly. In the present century, military governors in the provinces exerted absolute power over the Indians, only comparable to that exercised centuries before by the Spanish crown.

Wealthy Ladinos pressure the government to keep taxes low, while in the rural areas there are no schools, sewers and hospitals to serve a largely Indian population. A western diplomat pointed out recently that, in Guatemala, the distance between Indians and Ladinos is abysmal.

U.S. academicians have indicated that the cause of the country's political instability goes back to the 1954 *coup d'etat*. Guatemalan analysts differ. *Prensa Libre* columnist Jorge Guzmán wrote recently that the latest CIA scandal reminded him of the long history of foreigners who "invaded" Guatemala, beginning with the arrival of "thousands of Pizarros." The journalist wrote that "even Franciscan Diego de Landa, who lived among the

their own language, and dress in colorful garments. Almost all live in a small world with the village at its center. They grow corn and beans as the principal means of subsistence, although in the last few years heavy infrastructure investments are closing the gap between the indigenous and the Ladino worlds. This has prompted enormous social change in Guatemala.

2

Emerging from a Devastating Loss

Question: *Was there an important presence of the Marxist guerrillas in the Catholic university?*

Ramiro de León Carpio: Not at the beginning. I entered the university in 1966, not a very strong time for the guerrillas. The guerrillas had various moments, you see. The first one was when it emerged in the 60s in the eastern part of the country, only to fail by 1964. The guerrilla movement as such ended then, although other rebels revolted in the northern part of the country. These concentrated in the jungle, where conditions are more difficult. Later, in the mid-70s, they expanded to the mountains. They grew until the years 1980, 1981 and 1982, when a strong military threat became real.

When I arrived at Landivar University the most influential group at San Carlos university was the Patriotic Labor Youth (*Juventud Patriótica del Trabajo, JPT*) from which later stemmed a significant part of the guerrillas. There was less political activity at the Landivar campus. Although it had

Gen. Kjell Laugerud, who was in turn succeeded by Gen. Romeo Lucas García. But although there was no open confrontation with the university, there was general discontent because of social injustice and poverty, and constant electoral fraud. All of this generated protests in the university, but there was never the slightest thought of guerrilla participation, with the exception of a few who left the university to join the guerrillas.

Q: *How is it that while the country experienced an atmosphere of agitation, the university life you describe transpired so calmly?*

RDLC: There was calm in Landivar University, not in the state university. Landivar was founded under the condition that there would not be trouble. There was a degree of activity transcending to the community, but this was mainly academic, with art exhibits and other types of expression. Sometimes there were also protests, but not much more. The institution had kept pretty much to itself, making it clear to the students that the first priority was to study. As opposed to San Carlos, at Landivar any improper behavior was sanctioned.

Q: *While you were in the university you had to work to help support your family. What kind of work did you do?*

RDLC: I had to work from the first year to pay for my studies. First I worked at a court, but though the practice was interesting I didn't earn enough. I had just married and finally landed a job with the Ministry of Economy in its Department of Integration. Here I had the unique opportunity to be close to the Central American political process, first as an assistant adviser and later as an adviser. I became a member of a team that traveled making speeches to divulge the economic integration in the Central American common market. This practice was very helpful. I developed important contacts with economists and attorneys, although I was still only a student. Subsequently the Ministry of Economy transferred me to Congress, where all my tasks had to do with politics. This was 1970.

After I graduated I left Congress and began working as

an attorney in a law office, surrounded by colleagues specialized in commercial law. This was altogether different. We gave legal advice to large corporations and I began to excel as a lawyer.

Q: *Did you ever have your own law office?*

RDLC: In 1974, after four years of successful practice, I set up an office with another partner. We did pretty well. Meanwhile, my house began to fill with children. Ramiro and Jorge Eduardo came first. Then in 1976 Alejandro was born.

Q: *Was your law office untouched by the successive political crises that kept shaking up the country?*

RDLC: Of course not. I was very frustrated as a lawyer, which forced me to make a decision of extraordinary importance later in my life. In 1974 I was offered the position of secretary general of the State Council. This was a collegiate body of prominent persons and power groups that no longer exists. The concept had been copied from France. Although I was very young, my job carried a lot of responsibility. The council was composed of representatives from government, from San Carlos university, the Municipal Corporation, all business and financial sectors, and the unions. In other words, it was a highly political organism headed by the nation's vice president.

At that moment the vice president was Lic. Mario Sandoval Alarcón, a man of the extreme right. He had known me while I worked for Congress as a student. One day, when I was already practicing law, he telephoned me: "Ramiro," he said, "I know you don't share my ideas but you have experience in Congress and we need someone here who would be impartial and exercise good technical judgment. We need someone to manage the State Council."

I accepted. From the political standpoint, it was an extraordinary experience to be at the center of power. Though I was allowed to keep my law office, I devoted most of my time to the council, where I stayed four years. There I got to know many of the people who later held the highest offices in the nation. The representative of San Carlos university,

mists, teachers, union leaders, priests. Guatemala holds the world record of more priests murdered. The dead belonged to all professions, even businessmen.

Q: *It was during that period that kidnaping began, a practice that has caused so much trouble in Guatemala. Was any member of your family kidnaped?*

RDLC: There were many murders and kidnapings. They even kidnaped and murdered U.S. Ambassador John Gordon Mein. They gunned down Ambassador Count William Von Spretti, from Germany. Also many political leaders, like Manuel Colom Argueta; prominent businessmen, military chiefs, too many people.

Guatemala has had unique and sad experiences. It is estimated that over these 34 years 150,000 people were killed or disappeared. This has left some 100,000 widows and 250,000 orphans. One million people were dislodged, approximately 45 to 50,000 sought refuge in Mexico. Many of these are now returning. All wars are dirty, but ours has been one of the dirtiest.

It was indeed a war, though it is not officially called a war. In an attempt to hide the obvious, some experts prefer to describe it as "a low-intensity conflict." But it was a massacre. Some were tortured or wounded. Others were paralyzed. Thousands of soldiers were maimed. Guerrillas made ample use of a bomb they call *Quita pie* (Foot remover), which doesn't kill but destroys arms or feet. There are a lot of blind. The number of dead within the army ranks is known with relative certainty, but it's more difficult to know the dead among the guerrillas because they pick up their bodies and bury them. Many civilians died too.

Q: *You toured the country during those days of undeclared civil war. What did you see?*

RDLC: Probably my worst experience amid that climate of violence came later when my wife became ill and rapidly died of a blood disease. I was left a widower with three children of ages nine, seven and two. This changed my whole life.

Q: *What did that change bring to your life?*
RDLC: I lived through it as something awfully cruel, tremendously difficult. Our marriage was genuinely happy, very normal, truly special to me. So the outcome restrained my behavior. It held me back, completely paralyzed me. I loved my wife very much.
Q: *Was her death unexpected?*
RDLC: Not totally. Her illness had lasted two, three years. But the last year pointed to a fatal outcome. She was examined in Houston, Texas, where doctors predicted every chance of survival. It was a blood disease in which the defenses in the bloodstream turn into a threat to the body. A rare disease indeed, hard to treat, but one that only turned fatal if it affected a vital organ. Therefore, doctors in Houston assured us it wasn't so serious and she could even continue her pregnancy. In Guatemala doctors were of the opposite opinion. They insisted it was an incurable disease and warned us of a fatal outcome.

The opinion I got in Houston encouraged me to become a father again. My wife wanted very much to give me a daughter. We had three sons. Her pregnancy affected her body to the point of speeding up her death. In other words, her death on December 12, 1976, was unexpected in that during the prior two years she had been under extreme care and no one expected the worst. When it finally happened my children became the purpose of my life. They were very little. Caring for them forced me to retreat to a life at home, removed from the drama of the war in Guatemala. At that time I stayed away from all political activities, while I continued working in the State Council. Two years later, in 1978, there was a change in government. I didn't want to continue working for the administration, so I went back to my private law practice.

For two years I got involved in different things, among them giving legal counsel to various enterprises. My life changed again when I was offered the position of general manager with the Sugar Producers Association, the nation's

in life, that was a cycle that gradually declined into total disappearance. At the time I became an expert on sorrow and separation. I remember a book titled *La Separación de los Amantes* (The Separation of Lovers) by Igor Caruso, a South American writer, perhaps Chilean or Argentine, don't remember well. The topic was divorce in the American society. Someone recommended it to me and I recommended it to others. It's mostly about divorce, but it addresses the pain of separation, an issue of great grief to American society where many couples who have united their lives have had to separate overnight. The book explains how to overcome the consequences of separation. It helped me a lot.

When Anna Freud speaks about the defense mechanisms, for example, and describes what she calls "the delayed sorrow," she tells of people who only need six months to overcome separation. Women are particularly strong in dealing with separation, and, depending on the circumstances, some overcome it while others remain affected for the rest of their lives. I have known many widows and widowers whose pain was lighter than mine. It is the delayed or prolonged pain that is truly dangerous. Mine was more or less normal, according to my own final evaluation.

I reached an acute cycle from which pain began to decline. It was in the Sugar Producers Association where I started to let go. When my wife died we had just bought a beautiful house in the outskirts of the city. After she passed away it was impossible to continue living in it. I even remember the suffering of my older children. The day we buried her I tried to explain to the older kids what had happened, that she had become ill and God had not wanted her to continue suffering, etc. My second son started crying, but the older one asked questions. "Will we have a stepmother? Do we have to go live in the house so far away, the house we bought? Why can't we continue living downtown?" Those were his worries. About the stepmother I gave him a clear answer. I told him it was an ugly word that came from story books, and that we would talk about it later. In spite of my pain, I didn't want to swear, like other parents have done to their children, that I would never marry again. I think it's a mistake to make that kind of promise.

About the house, I decided to build a new one above my mother's house. I personally designed it, became an architect, a builder, and entertained myself all the time it took to finish it. It was a beautiful home made of mahogany and cedar, the finest woods in the world. I could have that luxury because I was the attorney of a wood enterprise that gave me the materials.

We were close to my mother and at the same time were independent. I remember one day, while talking to my children in our new beautiful wooden house, I heard birds chirping across the street where the owners of an alcohol company lived. They had many trees in their property. I went down and told my mother: "Have you noticed the beautiful day we're having today, and the lovely birds chirping in our neighbors' house?" She gave me a strange look and responded that all days were the same, that there were always birds in our neighborhood, and it was I who never stopped to notice. I looked at her and said, "I am cured, mother." I realized at that very moment that life goes on and you can't be paralyzed forever.

I remember that same day I gathered my children and told them that, yes, life was cruel and difficult, but above all it was also wonderful. They later told me they thought I had gone mad. But it was a defining moment in which I started anew. It was then I began to look at the world differently, becoming enthusiastic about work again, and deciding once more to get involved in politics and everything else that came afterward. Indeed, losing my wife was a tremendous experience, a trauma that hardened me and made me capable of enduring anything, including my stint with the sugar barons.

Q: *Did you come to admire any of the businessmen you worked with during those two years as manager of the sugar association?*

RDLC: From the business standpoint, yes. I worked with

3

Drafting a Constitution

Question: *During the early 1980s there was a succession of fraudulent governments, the military usurping power. What was your attitude toward them?*

Ramiro de León Carpio: I had reoriented my life, had finally come to understand I wasn't guilty of anything and had assimilated the loss of my wife as a turn of destiny. It may sound simple to those who have not experienced the loss of a deeply loved spouse. In 1984 I married my current wife.

During the 80s, full of life again, I was very close to my cousin, Jorge Carpio Nicolle, who was the editor of an important daily, *El Gráfico*. I was his private attorney and his company's legal counsel. We were also friends and saw each other a lot in those days. My wife liked him so much she insisted we asked him to be the godfather of our second child, as he was of the first one and later was to be of our third one as well. There was a strong identification in our approach to

they began to leave to get married. Jorge had an experience similar to mine, though he started out younger, at 18. An outstanding hard-working salesman, he built a successful business from scratch. He met every financial and business goal he had set for himself. And yet he constantly felt the calling to be a politician, although he had never taken part in politics.

Because of financial problems, Jorge could not even finish secondary school in Mexico. He had to catch up on his education here in Guatemala. Yet he became a very educated man. Traveled extensively. Spoke many languages. He was a true scholar. Art, history, cultural affairs, all these topics fascinated him. The only area in which he had never had experience was politics. And so when he decided to get into politics he had never spoken in public.

My grandmother loved him very much and they were truly close. I remember that when he told my grandmother that he was going to launch a newspaper, my grandmother told him, “Don’t do this. You are doing very well.” Which was true. He sold calendars all year round and he made a lot of money. Later he sold real estate and became extraordinarily rich. When he married, he went on a one-year-long honeymoon to Europe.

But my grandmother told him that a newspaper would push him to politics, to confrontation, and eventually to his death. She anticipated everything. She also told him that a newspaper would bring him failures and he was not used to failures. I remember she told him that it would hurt him. “Ramiro will not suffer too much, but you will,” she said. “You are accustomed to entrepreneurial success.” My grandmother was 90 years old and she predicted everything.

My grandmother’s advice was important. My family was a matriarchy and Jorge, even after becoming an important person, used to spend hours talking to her. He appreciated her wisdom.

Q: *Was there jealousy or rivalry between the two of you?*

RDLC: Not on my part. From the beginning it was clear that

Jorge Carpio was the leader. This changed afterward, however.

At the beginning my job was to travel throughout Guatemala and I was fascinated by everything I saw. In those early days I learned to love the countryside.

When we began to organize the party two positive elements had come together. I had experience from school, from the university, from the various jobs I had performed. Jorge contributed a colossal advertising and business background. For example, when we had to come up with a logo for the party, he sat down and shuffled ideas, many of which he had brought from Germany and Spain. Besides, he has an enterprise at his service, and with the help of one of his sons, for the first time a political party was advertised with the same techniques used commercially for selling a product.

Early on we decided that Jorge would stay on the sidelines, reserved for the right time to launch his candidacy, while I became general secretary. Popular reaction was excellent, though the logo was not well known. Our first challenge was to participate in the elections for the Constitutional Assembly in 1984. There was audacity in our move to form a political party to participate in elections to be held only eight months later. We won big, except that we could not penetrate as deeply as we had expected in the rural areas. Nationally the number of votes was the highest and it gave us the majority of the assembly's seats.

Q: *What was the reaction of the extreme forces that dominated the nation's politics, both from the right and from the guerrillas?*

RDLC: We took it from both sides. These attacks made us tremble. Of course, the extreme right, particularly the party National Liberation Movement (*Movimiento de Liberación Nacional, MLN*), was the first one to attack us and they did hit hard. And also the left. But the attacks only served to assure ourselves.

In August of 1983 the army commanders called Ríos Montt and asked him to retire. The purpose of Ríos Montt's coup was allegedly to remove the military from power and estab-

contender. Christian Democrats beat us in some areas, though we more or less ended up with a tie in the total calculation. We virtually buried the National Liberation Movement (MLN), the extreme-right political force. Its representation has since gone down to a mere symbolic presence of only three deputies. This was significant considering that since 1954 the MLN had been a big party, a constant source of controversy mainly due to its illegal introduction of weapons into the country. We also gave a hard beating to the Revolutionary Party, which represented the line of the October Revolution, the legacy of President Arévalo.

The elections on July 1, 1984, brought us our biggest triumph ever. A big win indeed for Jorge Carpio, and probably his only victory. Subsequently, he ran for president and lost. After a few partial victories he never could win the decisive battle. But we were able to gain a strong congressional representation while I became part of the Constitutional Assembly. Jorge stayed behind preparing himself for the presidential bid and playing a major role no one ever disputed, not me nor anyone else.

Q: *When did you become the alternate chairman of the Assembly?*
RDLC: Immediately. When I arrived at the Assembly I was an attorney who had devoted much time to the study of constitutional law and had become an expert. I had started studying the topic in Mexico, and later in Spain and in Guatemala. My doctoral thesis was an informed critical pedagogic paper titled "Doctrinal and Legal Analysis of the Constitution." So I was well trained for the Assembly work.

There were three forces — our party, National Center Union (UCN) with 23 deputies; the right-wing National Liberation Movement (MLN), with the support of the Institutional Democratic Party (PID) and the Nationalist Authentic Center (CAN), with similar numbers with 23; and the Christian Democrats with 22. In a very smart political move, we decided to join these other forces to form a block of 68 seats out of the total 88. Under this arrangement we created an alternate system in which the chairmanship was rotated among three persons elected among its members: Roberto Carpio Nicolle, the eldest of the Carpio brothers, representing the Christian Democrats; Héctor Aragón Quiñones, of the MLN; and myself, for UCN.

This development catapulted my political career. What had taken others 30 years, I had achieved in eight months. And being a lawyer gave me an edge over the others. Roberto Carpio was a great politician, as was Aragón Quiñones. But the issue in the Assembly was to draft the Constitution, the Electoral Law and the Habeas Corpus Law. A committee was formed for each of these pieces of legislation, and I requested to chair over the one that would work on the Constitution.

The alternate chairmanship was a unique format that rendered positive results with the drafting, despite all the political differences, of a new Constitution. We also agreed on a timetable to implement it, forcing the Chief of State and the military to approve it and allow the transition of power.

Q: *Are you referring to the so-called Committee of Thirty that drafted the present Constitution?*

RDLC: Of course. It was the Committee of Thirty and I chaired every one of its 103 sessions.

Q: *Do you believe that because of your work you have left a stronger imprint on the present Constitution than the rest of the politicians?*

RDLC: No doubt about it. First, because of my hard work. Second, because I became the life of the block we had formed with the Christian Democrats.

Q: *Was there a great affinity of ideas between your party and the Christian Democrats?*

RDLC: Yes, there was. But there was hard work. I arrived at the Assembly every morning at 7. After some administrative work I would chair the debates until the afternoon hours when the session with the Committee of Thirty began. Later I would take care of party issues, and at night I would meet with other fellow constitutional lawyers to discuss constitutional topics. Exhausting work. During that year and a half my children hardly saw me. I was still single. It was in De-

MLN, the PID and the CAN.

Q: *Granted that the military did not exert pressure, but the government must have been interested in knowing what was cooking in the Assembly. Was it not?*

RDLC: Of course. But there was freedom. What do I mean by this? The previous constitutions had been but repetitions of a recurring event: the coup d'etat. Every new constitution consistently followed a pattern set by the *de facto* powers of the moment. Not in our case. This Constitution was born with more freedom that the one in 1945, which is the best we've had. Our work was not governed by a group of jurists or intellectuals imposing their criteria, as was the case in 1945. We asked to be given freedom and the political circumstance allowed it. We had just come out of the coup and there was a well intended effort from segments of the military to do something durable and stable for the country.

The military were not very concerned about us. There were no extremists in the Assembly. The left was represented by the Christian Democrats, which at that time did not pose a danger.

To inform the government, Gen. Mejías Víctores served as liaison with the Chief of State. We met with him in a respectful atmosphere. It must be remembered that at that time we were the only legitimate body in the country. The rest — from the Chief of State to any ministry, judicial department, etc. — were temporary and not elected.

Q: *There wasn't pressure even when setting constitutional limits to the role of the military?*

RDLC: No. Had there been pressure the Assembly would have exploded. Even when we discussed the military there weren't big problems. We mentioned, for instance, that the Minister of Defense should be a civilian, which was out of the question at that moment. This explains why whenever I am asked if ours was the best Constitution, I reply that politics is the art of that which is possible, not of the impossible. At that specific moment, the Constitution we wrote represented the people's interests only to some extent. There were obviously some things impossible to accomplish under the circumstances.

Q: *Can you give me an example?*

RDLC: The one I just mentioned about the Minister of Defense being a civilian. Maybe in the future...

Q: *In Guatemala one of the most serious problems is human rights abuse. How did you approach this issue?*

RDLC: A good point. We turned the discussion around. Previous constitutions began establishing that Guatemala was a free nation, sovereign, independent, etc. and it went on to describe the structure of the government. Ours begins referring to the human person. The first two articles, as I have described before, start with the human being and the purpose and goals of the government to reach the common well-being. After the first two articles the text goes on to address two types of human rights — individual and social. The social rights in turn comprise economic, social and cultural rights. And for the first time we included a Decalogue of Human Rights.

This is when for the first time I got involved in human rights in its juridical dogmatic sense. Before, I had approached human rights based on the experience of living in this complicated country.

I know of very few constitutions which address human rights as well as ours does. Article 46, for example, is probably the most advanced piece of human rights legislation in the world. What really hurts us here is the implementation, the actual respect of human rights.

Our latest Constitution speaks of human rights rather than constitutional guarantees, which was the formula previously used to address the issue with white gloves. Besides, it addresses the family, culture. It guarantees land for the indigenous communities, which for the first time are mentioned in a constitutional text, and establishes ways to regulate this issue.

It speaks about education, about sports as a human right to recreation, about health, security, social welfare, the right

4

A Clean Party Goes Astray

Question: *What did writing the Constitution mean to you personally?*

RDLC: Like the issue of human rights, it has very much become part of my life. Because the other two Assembly co-chairmen were politicians and not lawyers, people associated me personally to the task and later referred to me as the ex-chairman.

To me it was a period of major accomplishment. Personally, I had overcome the sentimental crisis of my wife's death and had rebuilt my married life. Once my family was stabilized, I began to enjoy my work and wrote those constitutional articles as if I were making preparations for a trip. And since travel plans often turn out to be better than the trip itself, it was ideal.

Parallel to all of this was the political events in my life; the beautiful, Gothic side of politics that comes with organizing a new party, when it hasn't yet developed its ugly side of jealousy and such. In a stage where all is patriotic and nationalistic, it was also my period of maximum performance in politics. That, combined with writing the Constitution, the fundamental law of my country, made me work 18-20 hours a day with hardly feeling the effort.

We started working on the Constitution on August 1, 1983, and we finished it in less than a year and a half. It finally went into effect on January 14, 1985, coinciding with a new democratically elected government. Had I had my way I would have given the final document more of a social projection. It was precisely over this issue that I first had problems with Jorge Carpio.

Q: *Your cousin Jorge Carpio, the one who founded with you the UCN? Did he have any part in the drafting of the Constitution?*

RDLC: From outside of the Assembly, of course. As chairman of the Political Council of our party he took part in forums and, albeit indirectly, we discussed the big issues and the transformation.

You see, I had worked with him in the drafting of our party's statutes and in establishing its ideology. Our discussions turned very difficult. It was hard to defend pragmatism as the basis of centrism. What was the ideology? We were not at the right or left. Then what? We actually had a very rich ideology. All we needed was to link our ideology to the social philosophy of the Church, which like Marxism had everything — human rights, economics, social, judicial and political issues, etc.

Q: *Didn't the Christian Democrats sort of overlap your political space a bit at that time?*

RDLC: It did, though only formally. In the public's view we took a lot of space from their turf. Ours was the only party that in its first showing came out at the top places. In 1985, our second electoral experience, we challenged the Christian Democrats for the presidency and came out in second place, burying all other parties. The Christian Democrats had been, traditionally, the opposition party that had suffered harassment, exile, attacks from all prior governments. It was only natural for them to reach power, and they had a young team of politicians with good discourse, demagogic at times, but good and with a proper foundation.

Our party, with not a very creative leader, lacked clarity. It was never clear what we meant by being at the center. In politics it all depends what surrounds you. If I am at the center, for instance, with a Marxist at my left, I am therefore a rightist. Whereas if I have another centrist at my left I can tilt to the extreme right. It's the philosophy of praxis.

Q: *How did you approach difficult issues such as the guerrillas and the relationship with the military?*

RDLC: Our party was not confrontational. Our approach was pardon and national reconciliation toward all. Even forgetting, a word I later understood well and which isn't so easy to pronounce. To talk about pardoning and reconciling was the right thing then. To talk about forgetting, however, was more difficult. You can't force someone who has lived under terror to forget. But that was our position. Pardon and national reconciliation. To forget the past and move forward with a party for the future, with a new vision, new faces, new ideas, pragmatic, agile, and without confrontation.

We never had problems with the military because we had to justify nothing and could not be accused of anything. Besides, our position did not create problems to the right or to the left. Let's remember that Jorge Carpio belonged to the business sector. For reasons I never knew his colleagues were a little mistrustful of him. Maybe it was his personality. He didn't get along with other businessmen, even though he defended the principles of free market, etc. Which takes me back to the problems I myself had with him over the Constitution.

There were two issues. The fundamental one had to do with private property, an article debated for days and finally approved at 3 a.m. on the last plenary session. The tendency was to confer a social function to the concept of private property, an issue that's not even political any more and has become merely juridical. The business sector's propaganda then was that the Constitution would dictate that even a bicycle had to be shared with two or three other people, and that house owners had to share rooms with strangers. I of course did not share this approach. The final wording of the article merely says that the right to private property is respected. It fell under individual human rights as a right inherent to every person though it must benefit all. There was a lot of confusion over this.

Q: *And what did Jorge Carpio do?*

RDLC: Jorge was influenced by the business sector. He gave in to the pressure from the business sector and, as a consequence, our party yielded some space to the Christian Democrats. Jorge feared that we would lose support from the business sector and I ended up accepting his views, although I remained personally upset over the whole issue.

The second problem was the right of government employees to go on strike. Jorge and I reflected much over this issue. It was always my belief that a government employee had as much right to go on strike as a private employee. But from the standpoint of government there was concern about the obstacle a strike by government employees would pose to the governing function should a conflict be poorly handled. We had to regulate things in a way that the essential services would not be affected.

The country was amid heavy electoral activity. Both presidential candidates, Jorge Carpio and Vinicio Cerezo, opposed any special regulation on government employees. Curiously, their respective political parties supported the measure. The candidates did not want to upset some 200,000 government employees who could represent a little more than half-a-million votes. Jorge and I could never agree on this issue. Our party supported my actions and later identified itself with the Constitution.

Now it's different. Whoever manages today to regulate this type of strike is going to win votes, because the negative effects of the measure have been proven.

Q: *After the Constitution there was a presidential election in Guatemala, one of the few clean and democratic votes the country has* *ever known. Why did your party lose the election and what happened between you and Jorge Carpio?*

RDLC: When the Constitution was officially presented, presidential elections were called. They would follow the French model of absolute majority with runoffs. This was an improvement over the previous system of indirect election in which Congress had the final word if there was not a clear majority of one of the candidates. And, to put it bluntly, Congress was generally run by corrupt politicians, controlled and manipulated by the prevalent political mafia, who ended up determining who was to be president.

This changed with the new Constitution that established a different mechanism. First, the Electoral Commission that handled electoral results was abolished and replaced by a Electoral Supreme Court, which set up a totally transparent electoral procedure. With the institutional gear in place, we got ready to launch Jorge Carpio as our presidential candidate. At that moment, UCN remained well anchored at the center as a clean party. This is when my difficulties with Jorge began. They actually started with our quarrels over the party's ideology and political position. To the last moment I accepted and respected his position. There was never a desire on my part to take his place.

Halfway into the presidential campaign, Jorge was faced with the possibility of forming an alliance with the Revolutionary Party, which represented a certain segment of the left and had been involved in various financial scandals. It was a political force that could hurt our purpose and actions. An affiliation with it would have implied that we were joining forces that had before produced corrupt and ominous governments.

We had crushed the Revolutionary Party in the elections for the Constitutional Assembly, but with its little map the group at the moment still persuaded many people, including Jorge Carpio. To me it was a huge tactical mistake, a political aberration, and I opposed any association with the Revolutionary Party. It was over this issue that we had our first really important disagreement. Yet I finally gave in because the party's council accepted the alliance. It must not be forgotten that, with his authoritarian style, Jorge controlled the council.

Q: *What was Jorge Carpio's justification for such alliance?*

RDLC: His justification was that the alliance would be a winner. We lacked penetration in the rural areas of the country, and the Revolutionary Party supposedly had it. Although we had won, making inroads in the interior of the country had been difficult. From the public relations standpoint, it was not easy to make your party's candidates and symbols known to every voter.

Jorge's point was that a combination of a well-known symbol and new faces was a winning option. I was not alone in my opposition. Part of the UCN resisted alleging that the new faces were only on our side, while their side had people with dirty faces and bloody hands. I remember a psychologist at the university told me: "You had such a clean product, with difficulties to make it to the market, but clean." The product had the possibility of reaching people as it was — spotless. What they did was package it in dirty wrapping, blemished, filthy. Acceptable to many, but rejected by others. The irony is that the alliance never held and it was later dissolved.

Q: *Was it dissolved during the electoral campaign?*

RDLC: Yes. The vice-president we chose for the ticket was a man with a good reputation, a person who came out with good numbers in the polls, a politician who had once founded a party. A good friend who, later under my presidency, was appointed our ambassador to Mexico. But the party's internal problems got so bad that the Christian Democrats, very cleverly, managed to bombard the alliance and provoke the rupture on the verge of election day.

And then the worst happened. Not only was the alliance dissolved, but we ended up keeping some people from the Revolutionary Party who were accused of corruption. So we lost our party. There were also problems between Jorge and

Alejandro Maldonado.
Q: *Jealousy?*
RDLC: Personality problems. With all these problems the party lost the elections. I was traveling in Europe when I heard the news. I remember telling my wife that it all meant I had to incur in further sacrifices in light of the runoff.

The defeat cracked the party and we had to tour the country to explain why we lost and to reinforce the organization vis-a-vis the following electoral challenge in the runoff. Of course, as general secretary, I had to be the one offering the explanations.

When our vice-presidential candidate declined participating in the runoff, I was asked to place my name on the ticket. It was a tough political decision. I loved parliamentary politics and I could have waited to run for Congress. But I finally accepted the vice-presidential candidacy, knowing we were going to lose. Many criticized my decision and labeled it as "crazy" or "absurd." They too thought I should have run for Congress, and move on after five years there.

I have never regretted the decision. It allowed me to become better known nationally. I needed to be more popular if I was to have a political future. Besides, the party was very near to me and I felt I couldn't leave Jorge alone. It was a sacrificial play that had its price at the time but later would yield some benefits. I campaigned with much dignity, visiting all districts with Jorge.

Many mistakes were made. I have always believed you don't lose an election unless you make mistakes. You can start with a high percentage in the polls and then lose because of mistakes. There were many mistakes in this election, as well as attitude problems, such as the whole issue of the alliance.
Q: *Weren't you prepared for defeat by then?*
RDLC: Of course. We knew we were going to lose. The problem was how to come out of the election in one piece and not lose our skin in the process. The political climate helped us. For the first time in years Guatemala had a democratically

elected president. Personally, I came out looking good from the results announced by the Electoral Supreme Court. I remember the photo shaking the winner's hand before the outgoing president. It marked the end of an era in the history of Guatemala after a long and terrible process. Unfortunately, the newly elected president, Vinicio Cerezo, never rose to the occasion. He arrived at the presidency loaded with popularity and international support, called to lead in a country with a stable economy and an enviable political situation — all that a new president yearns for. Yet Cerezo was a total failure. Not only corruption, but poor management and lack of leadership led his administration to disaster. I don't want to get into details, but people felt totally deceived. There was a widespread sense that a great opportunity was missed.

This environment gave us — UCN, Jorge Carpio, myself — a viable political space from which we could lead a constructive, serious opposition, aiming at a potential victory five years later. Jorge realized he had possibilities and began working hard. Unfortunately, again he made a series of mistakes that pit him against a segment of our parliamentary representation. I talked to him and asked him not to pay attention to gossip and rumors. Although my own political figure had grown, I had never attempted to change Jorge. There was mistrust between us, however. Furthermore, the party had taken some ideological avenues I didn't share completely.

Q: *How would you describe this ideological change?*

RDLC: In the first place, the purity with which the party had been born was lost. There was a mixture of people who did not accept dialogue. People overwhelmed with all kinds of problems and who I thought didn't belong in our party. These were individuals with very ambiguous politics and ideology. They dreaded the Christian Democrats and made them a target of constant attacks. A very destructive attitude that only benefited the Christian Democrats. With a different attitude we would have reached power easily and in no time.

I was always very frank and open, something Jorge always appreciated. One day, on our way back from a trip to Peru, I told him: “Look. I am the party’s general secretary and I don’t like what’s going on between us. The best way to deal with this is that you take full charge and assume the responsibilities of general secretary.” He was moved. “Ramiro,” he said, “I’m sorry for what’s happened. Please forgive me for mistrusting you. You have taught me a lesson.” It was incredible. With tears in his eyes he told me that I had made him very happy.

And here’s something interesting about Jorge Carpio. One day I ran into a few of my former university students on the streets who told me they had drawn a political curve about me. “What’s that?” I asked them. They explained that instead of moving forward I was moving backward; that in a month's time I had gone from chairman of the Constitutional Assembly to a non-person without even moving into Congress. That I had agreed to being a vice-presidential candidate on a losing ticket while I could have been leading the parliamentary group. Furthermore, I was demoted to deputy general secretary. These students had drawn what they called the “curve” of my political activity. It showed the trajectory from the party’s general secretary, chairman of the Constitutional Assembly, and chairman of the Committee of Thirty, down to non-elected vice-president...

Q: *Did you take this badly?*

RDLC: No. It helped me take a realistic look at my political career. Curiously, the study showed that as I lost positions my popularity and credibility increased. The two lines crossed: one ascending in credibility, knowledge, charisma and public acceptance; the other, marking institutional positions, going downward.

My subsequent resignation from the party occurred without a fight, which was unprecedented in our environment. People used to leave arguing, insulting. I just had a good conversation with Jorge. He had not complied with some of our agreements, but I didn’t mind. I left and concentrated on my profession. In the balance, the student's "curve" turned out to be interesting. I saw clearly that, in politics, failure was not all that negative. All the contrary, it boosted popularity.

Jorge knew my departure was going to hurt him. I had gained prestige as the Assembly chairman, had the reputation of being an honest person, a good speaker, a solid debater on television, etc. He was not a good speaker himself. He had a temper and often lost control.

Early on I was his confidant, and he would consult me and ask for my feedback on specific issues. I would advise him to be prudent, would comment on things he should have done differently, etc. This continued during the first few years. And then he began listening to the adulation of others.

I always told Jorge the truth. If he had been okay, I'd tell him. When he made mistakes, I also told him. But the people who surrounded him only praised him and my negative feedback sounded off key. I continued to do it, nonetheless, until in a public debate President Cerezo employed his usual cleverness to crush Jorge. One has to admit the President was smart, had charisma, charm and a lot of experience. Vinicio has been in politics since his early youth and had the cunning Jorge never had. So after this public debate, in which Cerezo made Jorge lose his temper, Jorge asked me what I thought. I told him it had not been good, and as I was elaborating that he shouldn't have lost his temper, his daughter-in-law came to tell him he had been "marvelous, very good!" Other party members and relatives joined the group to tell him he had been "great." "You really crushed him to pieces," said a family member.

Upon hearing these things I began to withdraw. Jorge was talking with my wife and we left through the back door. Outside my wife told me, "Let's go home and celebrate." "Celebrate what?" I responded. There was really nothing to celebrate. But we went for a few drinks and I was upset because I knew it had not gone well. At a party in the house it was incredible. People watched the tape of the debate and repeatedly told him how he had actually pulverized his opponent. Totally unreal! Since that moment I opted not to comment on his public performance anymore lest I continued to be perceived as the movie's villain.

I withdrew and stopped writing Jorge's speeches. This thing about the speeches was funny because there had come a time sometime before when my speech-writing was no longer trusted and I had begun using a third person, someone closer to him ideologically, who would present it to him as his. Then Jorge would come to me and ask me, "What do you think of this?" And I would approve or correct some line, in my own writing! All to continue helping him without hurting him.

Approximately two years after the electoral defeat, I again talked to him honestly to make two points. One, I wanted out of the party altogether. I told him I didn't want to continue being his political shadow, especially after having been demoted to deputy general secretary. Secondly, I suggested he change the party line to a more rational discourse or face total failure. He didn't want me to leave, but the conditions for staying were unacceptable and I finally left together with other valuable party members. My predictions on the fate of the party, by the way, eventually became reality.

So my party politics ended without a feud, without attacking Jorge. I left without much noise. The media respected us and didn't turn it into a big deal.

Q: *While the principal opposition party, the UCN, dissolved, what was happening in government? What was President Cerezo up to?*

RDLC: As I've mentioned, during the first two years of Cerezo's term the country saw economic growth. The administration later lost credibility after instances of corruption and other business. On the other hand, guerrilla activity escalated, probably encouraged by what was happening in Nicaragua and El Salvador.

The economy started its decline exactly halfway into the presidential term. Economic instability went hand in hand with political instability, and the resulting situation, compounded by corruption and the guerrilla escalation, drew a highly preoccupying picture. After Cerezo's first two years of change solutions slipped away and later it became too late...

Q: *In other words, political instability was reborn, but, didn't Cerezo waste an opportunity to restrain the military with bolder actions from the government?*

RDLC: With the popular and international support he enjoyed in the first few months Vinicio Cerezo could have done anything he wanted and put some order in the country. But he didn't. And when he tried to catch up, it was too late. His weakness had become so huge by then that all he managed to do was keep the status quo.

Q: *Was there a fear that the democratic regime would collapse?*

RDLC: Of course. In May of 1988, exactly halfway into the term, there came the first coup attempt. There was wide decomposition.

I was in France with my wife when that first attempt occurred. When I heard the news in the middle of a convention of liberal parties in Paris I wired all Guatemalan media denouncing the coup attempt and demanding the continuation of the constitutional government that had been installed by popular vote. When I returned a very nervous Jorge Carpio met me at the airport. Before I got a chance to talk to the media he told me my telegram had not been well received. Apparently, mine had been the only public reaction against the coup. No one had protested; not even in Congress. The situation was so critical that no one reacted. People didn't care. Civic education was low and people were not used to defending democracy. It was different later, during the presidency of Jorge Serrano Elías, when we all stood up and defended democracy.

Civic education wasn't any better with Jorge Carpio and UCN. They protested saying I had come out to defend the Christian Democrats. They failed to understand that I was supporting democracy. I wasn't defending the Christian

Democrats; I stood up for whoever represented the Constitutional government. Inconceivably, UCN didn't react until after I had returned from Paris, and it was too late then.

In May of 1989 there was another coup attempt. It was again aborted, but by then the military had become a pilar of government.

Q: *Was that when the house of the Defense Minister was militarily occupied?*

RDLC: There was an enormous internal decomposition in the country. It was partly attributed to the tax reform, which had not gone half as far as it later went under my administration. The proposal for tax reform caused serious trouble to President Cerezo. The business sector went all out against him. Old wars were unearthed, and they launched a campaign saying the President had made a shift to the extreme left.

Some businessmen began accusing cabinet members of being ex guerrillas. I never accepted this behavior. They also accused the President's wife, Raquel Blandón de Cerezo, of being an extremist. President Cerezo was hurt by not making the right decisions during his first years. After two coup attempts, the situation relied on the support from the military. The Defense Minister, Gen. Héctor Gramajo, did his best to avoid another coup and any further interruption of the democratic normalcy by the military. Gramajo defended the administration and sent a few officers to jail.

There were great expectations that Cerezo's government was going to fight poverty and corruption. It never happened. He didn't even sit down with the guerrillas to agree on a cease-fire and negotiate peace. Additionally, the situation in Nicaragua hurt his administration, as did the confrontation with the United States over human rights violations.

The positive element of Cerezo's term was the peace initiative in Central America — in Nicaragua and El Salvador. The Cold War was not over. There was armed struggle linked to Cuba, with financial aid coming from Havana to the Sandinistas and to the Salvadoran guerrillas.

Q: *Sandinism penetrated Guatemala, didn't it? It found ways to feed the guerrillas?*

RDLC: Absolutely.

Q: *Did it create instability in the Guatemalan government?*

RDLC: Not at the government level because there was an attitude of neutrality in President Cerezo's foreign policy, which ended up pitting the President against the United States. Guatemala opposed the invasion of Nicaragua and neutrality was uncomfortable and inconvenient to Washington. The United States favored confrontation, and Cerezo was placed in a weak position internally when he lost U.S. support. This caused much internal pressure, which compounded by human rights violations placed Guatemala again on the international spotlight. The international community overwhelmingly turned against the Guatemalan government. Cerezo began to have problems with broad segments of the population over human rights violations and government corruption. With business his troubles resulted from official embezzlement and mafia-like confrontations.

Against the backdrop of a complex moment in Central America, where the links between the Salvadoran and the Guatemalan guerrillas loomed large, the Cerezo administration faced coup attempts, experienced instability, and was hurt by people's disillusion.

In geopolitical terms, it was fortunate that, for Cold War reasons, Central America stayed on the U.S. agenda and continued being an important issue to the international community.

Q: *Are you saying that when you became Human Rights Commissioner Guatemala was going through a terrible time?*

RDLC: When I abandoned politics and left the party, I founded the Atanasio Tzul Institute, an organization named after an indigenous leader, a harbinger of our independence heroes who confronted the Spaniards and preferred dying than living in slavery.

Through this institution I tried to educate people on civic and democratic issues. I wrote a small book titled "Constitutional Catechism," explaining our Constitution briefly and in simple terms. I elaborated especially on the part about people's human rights so that, knowing their rights, they could defend themselves from any violation. As president of this institute I received international aid from Europe, from world institutions, democratic figures in the United States, Canada, etc.

I also devoted time to university teaching from 1986 to 1989. I focused on Constitutional Law and Political Science, topics I always loved. My contacts with young students stimulated me to embrace ideals again and participate, albeit at faculty level. Not wanting any part in political organizations, I only agreed to represent the faculty before the University High Council.

Q: *Are you referring to the Jesuit university? Didn't you feel any rancor toward the Jesuits for expelling you from school?*

RDLC: For better or worse, the Jesuits have always been a constant in my life. I didn't hold any hard feelings against them for expelling me. To the point that my own children attended Jesuit schools. Two of my children actually graduated from this university. The youngest didn't because he was expelled pretty much like I was. At some point I also served as president of the parents' organization. And, yes, later as a professor things were again difficult.

But as a professor I devoted much of my time to go over textbooks and debate with students. I learned a lot and had no real problems with the Jesuits. During that time I divided my time between the university and my family. My work at the Constitutional Assembly had given me a name and it led to much traveling, within the country and abroad. Also the institute I founded had great accomplishments and my book on the Constitution had large circulation. Everywhere I went someone came up with a copy in his hands asking for my autograph or discussing its contents. Indians, peasants, people who had returned to the country asked me about the Constitution. It was a truly flattering period of my life.

5

The Human Rights Commissioner

Question: *How did your position as Human Rights Commissioner fit in with the institutional shortcomings of Guatemala's democracy? What credibility could it have in such a context?*
Ramiro de León Carpio: The Constitution created the position following other advanced charters established in Nordic nations and Spain. Of course, there were also contributions of our own since human rights violations is a significant Guatemalan issue.

After abandoning politics I remained closely linked to the human rights issue, particularly in its possible relation to the Constitution. Because of my attitude, my way of thinking and acting, I gravitated toward this issue. Besides, my Constitutional Catechism became an important working tool for the 50,000 teachers and the 10,000 schools in Guatemala.

In the era of democratic stabilization under President Vinicio Cerezo the nation had in place as basic institutions a Constitutional Court, an Electoral Supreme Court and the position of Human Rights Commissioner. The first two had essential functions. The electoral high court, for example, as a guarantee for free elections. Since our Constitution was approved all our elections have been clean. It may sound obvious in any other place in the world, but in Guatemala it has been achieved at a high cost. The other two institutions have also had honest, effective performances.

As to the Human Rights Commissioner, it took a lot to get this institution to work. We must not forget that under Vinicio Cerezo there was a period of serious violations of people's liberties. There were, as I explained earlier, much arbitrariness.

It was understandably difficult to establish the concept of a Human Rights Commissioner at the very same time human rights were being violated. Finally, in 1987, the name of an elderly university professor, Gonzalo Menéndez de la Riva, who had been a member of the Electoral Supreme Court, was discussed. He was a good academician who knew the law well.

Menéndez de la Riva thus became our first Human Rights Commissioner and remained in the job during 1988 and 1989. After completing two of the five-year-term the Constitution had established for the Commissioner, he resigned at the end of 1989 after an argument with President Cerezo, although the official reasons given were poor health and advanced age.

Because there were still three years left on his term, there was an intense search for his replacement. Another professor's name came up as a candidate. But in spite of his credentials and his solid reputation, my name was also proposed at the suggestion of the international community, the Church, and other popular sectors. At the moment I didn't belong to any political party.

Q: *What was the nomination process like?*

RDLC: It was tough. The Commissioner is expected to meet rigorous requisites similar to those required for Supreme Court members. He must be an attorney and a notary, must be older than 40 and have more than 15 years of service, plus a high lifetime reputation.

His name must be presented by Congress's Human Rights Committee, which gathers representatives from all parties holding seats in the legislative body. They come up with three names and a plenary vote is called. The reason he is elected by Congress is to detach his functions from the executive branch of government. His status is equivalent to a member of Congress, although he is given absolute autonomy and independence. And he must present an annual report to Congress on the status of human rights in Guatemala.

As a champion of the people and a representative of Congress, which in turn represents the people, the Commissioner's primary job is to protect the human rights guaranteed by the Constitution during the five-year term for which he is elected. His second function is to investigate and report on any administrative behavior that may hurt the people's interests. In fact, he is free to investigate whatever he deems necessary.

His third task is to hear accusations anyone wishes to make about human rights violations. This is where most of my time went. The Commissioner is expected to demand, privately or publicly, corrective measures from government officials on the cases presented to them. And he could always publicly denounce any wrongdoing.

To me it was one more challenge in my life. A difficult option, really. I knew there was an academic angle to the work, but there was another associated to more practical situations that was going to spell trouble for me. I had tried to educate the population, which was comfortable and satisfying to me, and was easy in Guatemala where nothing had been done before in this area. But it was the other part — the defense, the investigations, the accusations and denunciations, the resolutions that, although moral, were important and could have more devastating effects than judicial sanctions — that was more difficult.

Q: *You mean there were life-threatening risks?*

RDLC: It had a high risk due to circumstances in Guatemala, which ironically had been my argument all along for making it a priority.

Q: *How were you perceived among the powers-that-be in the country — the military and the businessmen? Did they see you as a leftist?*

RDLC: Perhaps. Some businessmen saw me as a man of liberal ideas, politically to the left, albeit a moderate left, a left-to-center position.

Q: *Did you agree with that perception?*

RDLC: I'd say yes. I don't believe much in political colors. I never trust labels. You either perform or you don't. Things get done or they don't, whether the label is liberal, socialist, whatever. Having said that, I believe I did have a certain leftist way of thinking. Although the support I gained to all my attitudes came actually from my honesty. I was as honest as my predecessor, only younger. To me, honesty means to respond to the people's interests.

The powers-that-be saw me with fear, with resentment, with preoccupation. They feared that once in the job I would develop a style not of their liking. And because I was younger, the fear was stronger. Yet they ended up accepting me, because there were major improvements despite the violence and the guerrillas.

Q: *And what did the guerrillas have to say about all this?*

RDLC: The guerrillas attacked the entire establishment. They had emerged as anti-establishment and had rejected participation in the Constitutional Assembly, which left them out of the constitutional game. To the guerrillas everything had an evil mark, even the way the constitutional document was written. To this day they have not accepted it simply because they had no part in it. All other political, philosophical and ideological forces that had a role in the legal system at the time, participated. Of course, the 1945 Constitution directly forbade the participation of communist organizations in elections. This had been changed to totalitarian organizations, but it was all the same prohibition. Our Constitution changed all that. It eliminated that article and today all organizations can participate.

The guerrillas have never acknowledged it. They see the Constitution as illegitimate, as part of an establishment they wish to modify, destroy. This despite the risks taken and the honesty with which it was accomplished. Although they did not make a statement when I was elected, after some time they aired much criticism alleging I did not take action.

Q: *How did you go about your work? Say a lady came to your office and told you in such and such a place atrocities were occurring. What did you do?*

RDLC: First of all, I responded to organized entities with some credibility. And I never felt alone in my performance. The people and the media were always with me. I always had the support of the press. Not only with coverage, but with actual backing. Maybe this is what saved me from popular organizations and from the general population. I also enjoyed international support. I had a good relationship with the U.S. ambassador, with the representatives of the European Union, the Canadian and the Mexican ambassadors, and from other Latin American countries. It was this international support that protected my life and prevented assassination attempts.

Q: *Were there serious attempts on your life?*

RDLC: No, not actual attempts. The normal threats in Guatemala, where threats constitute a national vice and people are accustomed to living in fear. I personally didn't go through anything grave. My people did. I am referring to other officials. But it was never a serious problem for an institution that lured a lot of respect. It was perhaps that all those involved in violence and threats knew that if anyone abused them they could come to us and claim justice.

There was risk nonetheless. The main function of the Commissioner is to make sure government institutions do not abuse, and in that sense we organized ourselves to hear and investigate every accusation. The police, for example. To investigate any possible violation they incurred we created an investigating procedure, and with the help of international organizations we obtained the services of a laboratory. Not to gather evidence, which belonged in the criminal justice system, but simply to make sure we could make proper verification before ruling or accusing any individual or institution.

I remember many international meetings of human rights champions where there was an impressive exchange of ideas. On one occasion, at an international conference in Mexico, I spoke after a representative from Great Britain who said his primary task was to oversee human rights abuse of the elderly. He had a team who visited old ladies and men at hospitals. When my turn to speak came the contrast was huge.

On another occasion, in Europe, I sat at a table over lunch with the representative from Sweden. This person told me the most serious violation he was investigating was an accusation from a school where a female teacher dressed in a Muslim habit, and that, of course, was unacceptable. He went to explain it was discriminatory. Imagine how terrible to show up like that where there were Catholic students, Jews, Protestants, etc. I just nodded and said, half-jokingly, that it was indeed a serious case of discrimination.

And there was this Canadian who also had a case of discrimination — in Toronto or nationwide, I don't remember well — due to a law forbidding bars to open on holidays while it failed to mention stores where liquor was sold at higher prices. Those high-price stores were available to those who could pay. What discrimination!

So, hearing this, I told them: "In Guatemala we really don't have any serious discrimination in bars nor abuses against the elderly. What we have are people kidnaped, disappeared, tortured, that kind of thing."

Of course, it doesn't mean human rights were not important in all those countries. In my speech in the last international human rights meeting I said each nation had its own culture and characteristics and it had to act depending on the degree of respect for human rights that existed, be it

Sweden or Guatemala.

During my tenure as commissioner I had a lot of contact with my equivalent in Spain. He helped me a lot with seminaries, technical cooperation, etc. I also had contact with other Europeans. The representative from Finland, for instance. In our conversation I asked him what was the worst confrontation he had had with his government. He responded he had to denounce a vice minister who by mistake had lost a small amount of government money. Then I asked him for something more difficult, with the police, for example. He thought for a few minutes and finally said: "Of course. We have had many problems with the police. You see, in Finland police officers are loved and respected, and there have been times they have been forced to work longer hours and, though they make good money, we have been asked to demand more salary for them so they are not exploited."

I have mentioned these cases to make the point of how enormously different things were in Guatemala from many other countries. The moment came in Guatemala when the Human Rights Commissioner had a better reputation than Amnesty International. He made a difference. We worked with the truth and we unraveled many specific cases of extrajudicial deaths. And for the first time the guerrillas were also pointed out as human rights abusers.

My investigations prompted people to accept that not only the government violated human rights but individuals as well. I was thus given power to point to private citizens outside of government for human rights abuse in addition to whatever other criminal implication their action may have had and its resulting legal conviction under the law.

With such authority I could for the first time charge the Guatemalan National Revolutionary Union (UNRG), official name of the guerrilla movement, with concrete violations, like blowing up the Moca bridge where two people were killed, one of them a doctor. I went to the place and my investigation led to a guerrilla faction that was part of UNRG. For the first time our nation, based on accurate facts, was able to justly charge the guerrillas for violating the human right to life, to physical integrity, to economic status.

Q: *Which were the more important cases you handled in those years?*

RDLC: The first one among the pending cases was a massacre in El Aguacate. It was difficult because it had happened a year before.

Q: *Is El Aguacate a village?*

RDLC: Yes. A village in the Department of Chimaltenango, an indigenous zone. The massacre was a highly political case in 1988. When I studied the details I decided not to condemn anyone. This was one of my first decisions, and I made it contrary to all the pressure to condemn the military. I couldn't do that because there was also an accusation against the guerrillas and the facts weren't clear. When I got the case too much time had elapsed and there was not enough evidence to charge anyone in particular. It was a demonstration of objectivity, equanimity and impartial judgment. Although my decision was not of everyone's liking, I was beginning to be perceived as an unbiased official who didn't take sides.

The year 1990 passed with only minor problems. Then came the case that brought the spotlight on the Human Rights Commissioner, an incident in Santiago Atitlán on December 1. The tension had been escalating since the civilian population had accused the military of abuse. There was action, rebellion and finally heavy friction between the military and the people. That night there was an incident with an officer. People got up in the middle of the night, tolled the bells, and marched en masse toward the military headquarters. Once there, they became nervous. The soldiers opened fire and killed more than twenty people.

I was called and a few hours later I was in the place collecting facts. I condemned one individual and also issued an institutional condemnation. It was a practical resolution demanding the immediate withdrawal of the military from the village. My ruling impacted the nation and the international community and the case became my test of fire. Since that resolution the Human Rights Commissioner reached his cred-

ibility peak and obtained widespread support.
Q: *Were the military angry?*
RDLC: They reacted very defensively. And so did President Cerezo. However, my ruling was simply accepted and the military withdrew immediately. Of course, they alleged guerrilla infiltration, but for the first time the military assumed responsibility and the culprits were convicted. For the first time in the history of Guatemala, a court sentenced one soldier to a 15-year term, and two others to three- and four-year terms. The moral condemnation had an enormous effect on the case.

Later, as president, I understood how hard it must have been for Vinicio Cerezo. The massacre occurred at the end of his presidential term and left a very bitter taste. It was a tough resolution and the military had to withdraw, which later brought about other repercussions when the area turned into a passageway for the guerrillas.

That was not the only incident in Santiago Atitlán. Months later a police unit had to be assigned to the town, which had been left without any authorities on site. One night a police officer from another municipality arrived chasing a criminal. Again residents got nervous, bells were tolled, and the problem turned serious. People marched and surrounded the police building. The officers responded hurling tear-gas grenades that almost asphyxiated some of the demonstrators. When things got really bad, I was again called in the middle of the night. I hopped on a helicopter and was there in the first hours of the following morning.

The situation was totally different from the previous occasion. This time the lives of police were in peril. I had to confront the indigenous population that, because it was Saturday, was partying and under the influence of alcoholic beverages. They were very excited and talked about lynching officers. I faced them and had to yell at them, at times through an interpreter though the majority spoke Spanish. I warned them that I was going to escort the officers through town on their way out and, if anyone dared to launch any attack against them, all their social gains would be reversed. I told them that if the officers were found guilty of any crime, the courts would convict them.

This was probably my most difficult speech ever. And also one of the most stimulating because lives were saved. There were thousands of people there, all under the effects of alcohol. They belonged to the Tzutuhile tribe, demonstrably the most violent and warring race of all. It was tense to come down from my speech before the whole population gathered in church and start walking through the crowd escorting the officers. Of course, they yelled claiming the officers deserved to be killed, but I kept reprimanding them and calming the officers, imposing my personality while fearing someone would throw a rock or other hard object at us. I finally took the officers to a boat and we abandoned the village safely.

I was involved for a third time yet in events in Santiago Atitlán. I had received the visit of the United Nations human rights expert, my friend Prof. Christian Tomushat. I took him to Santiago Atitlán to show him one of our most conflictive areas. There we were told that peasants could not go to the fields to work due to the violent encounters between the guerrillas and the military. They shot at anything that moved in the fields.

People stayed at home in absolute misery because they could not cultivate the land. They couldn't even pick up the dead on the fields fearing they were traps set by the guerrillas. I mention this only to illustrate the terror under which many Guatemalans were forced to live. These were years of hard work for us. Many cases had to be investigated — some of a political nature, others simply criminal. I remember a group of prisoners who had been tortured by the police. I had to issue institutional condemnations. Had to explain that torturing was illegal and immoral.

6

A Coup from the Palace

Question: *Was Serrano Elías already in power when these incidents in Santiago Atitlán occurred?*

Ramiro de León Carpio: These were the years from 1988 to 1992. Serrano assumed the presidency in 1991. I had more problems with Serrano than with Cerezo. Under the Cerezo Administration there was never pressure, a complaint, a messenger — nothing. He accepted my rulings, responded to them, but never resorted to intimidation. President Cerezo always maintained his democratic performance. He took the blows, if you will; assimilated the difficult resolutions.

Not so with President Serrano. President Serrano openly blasted the Human Rights Commissioner and said whatever came to his mind, from insults to threats, before his cabinet, members of his government and the chiefs of staff. It made no difference to me. I had built a solid institution devoted to saving human lives. The first time we saved a life, literally rescued someone from death, it was clear to me that creating the position of Human Rights Commissioner and my taking that difficult job were worth all the trouble. Life is the most sacred gift God has given us. The possibility of saving a life encouraged me to continue working, feeling myself necessary to many helpless people who called on me because their individual rights — their freedom, their integrity — had been violated.

Q: *Tell us about that first life that was saved. What were the circumstances?*

RDLC: It was a very special case, with an angle of mistaken identity. We were told someone was unjustly being held by the authorities. I investigated and personally took up the issue with the highest military authority. I showed up at the place where he was being held charged with subversion. It was the 25th of December. I warned the military that if that person appeared unharmed within hours I would dismiss the case. But to stand ready for the consequences if he didn't. In those days it was realistic to consider such case as a life-or-death instance.

There was a lot of confusion. Apparently the military had hastened and arrested the wrong person. His wife and children were in my office with unequivocal proof that he was innocent. The military reacted and he was released without a bruise.

There were other similar cases. The commissioner gained the trust of many, and people were delivered to my custody even by the military. Persons linked to the guerrillas. I remember a woman whose last name was Ortiz.

Q: *Diana Ortiz?*

RDLC: No, it wasn't Diana. I think her name was Verónica, a guerrilla fighter brought to my custody by the military. And there were others. Some of them returned to a normal life; others disappeared in the mountains. But all saved their lives and the law was applied.

Q: *Wasn't it an illusion to try to improve the human rights situation in the middle of a war that had claimed many lives and in which many others had disappeared?*

RDLC: Certainly. I've always said the primary cause of human rights violations is war. Neither side wants to lose a war. Particularly in a guerrilla confrontation in which groups operate outside the law and anti-government forces challenge a legitimate constitutional army called to protect the peace, sovereignty and tranquility of the citizens.

Of course, I've never heard of a war without excesses from both sides. The Vietnam War was not exactly a model of a clean war for the United States. France has little good to say about its confrontation over Algeria. The Spaniards did not have a gentlemen's war in Cuba. There are no clean wars. It's the same in Guatemala.

In 1992, however, I came up with a different approach to human rights. Peace talks had already started and, considering that if the armed struggle were resolved there would still be other areas of violations, I launched a campaign to address other rights, such as social justice, education, work, housing, health care, infant mortality, etc. It was just as painful to die from wounds caused by a weapon or a terrorist artifact as from inanition, starvation, lack of medical attention. Or to suffer poverty, misery, exploitation, discrimination. I surveyed all social segments in the country, indigenous and non-indigenous, and came up with suggestions to resolve these other problems.

Some people were concerned with this message, although it was mostly seen with objectivity and as a very pressing issue.

Q: *Do you believe some conservative sectors perceived someone who spoke of indigenous rights necessarily as an enemy of their interests?*

RDLC: Of course. But the majority of people saw it as the only way out. In 1995, for instance, four guerrilla commanders turned themselves in. They were interrogated and, after they offered a lot of information, were pardoned. In a conversation one of them told me their banner was no longer ideological nor Marxist. "I've never heard of Marx," he told me. "I would have never understood. The reason I joined the guerrillas was that I am poor. I was in total anguish. Fighting in the mountains was my way to try to improve the social and economic situation of my country."

He went on to say that what I am doing from the presidency — taking electricity, running water, and especially hope to the people — was to them worse than a bullet. He used that phrase. It was like taking away their banner, he added. The peasants they recruited, he said, were hopeless people to whom they offered change. If these people saw the President as an honest man who would give them electricity and water, they would hope to eventually have a school, a teacher, a highway, a bridge, etc.

The indigenous leaders reacted similarly. Guatemala had just established the Indigenous Development Fund when an indigenous leader approached me and said, "If you continue working in this direction, we will find a balance between the socio-economic development and our indigenous cultural identity. We will not be faced with the option that to improve our life we have to stop being Indians."

Peace is worthless if we don't make it durable. When I was commissioner the voice wasn't heard. In 1995, it was heard and there was some sense of organization in the indigenous communities.

Q: *I imagine one of the biggest problems in your term as Human Rights Commissioner was the self-coup President Serrano Elías enacted from the presidency in 1993. Tell us about that interruption of Constitutional normalcy.*

RDLC: Let me remind you that in 1992 I accepted a second term as commissioner. There had been much speculation about my political plans and many placed me as a natural candidate for the future. I had obtained renown as commissioner and had three years — 1993, 1994 and 1995 — to work on my candidacy. My reelection to a second term as commissioner, however, implied I was declining any electoral aspirations. The fact was I was highly disappointed over partisan politics and was working on something I loved, serving others. I didn't feel I necessarily had to be the nation's president to make a political contribution to my country. I was doing a good job as commissioner and decided to stay there and pursue my plans to strengthen the institution, making it grow in many ways, particularly in the new area of collective rights.

The nation's internal political crisis reached its peak in 1993. President Serrano made many mistakes, one of them getting carried away by corruption and greed. He began to misuse the millions assigned to confidential presidential expenses and followed Congress's corrupt stream.

As senator, Serrano had sworn never to commit extorsion, much less to bribe deputies. Yet he eventually did and it led him to despair and anxiety. Heading in the wrong direction, Serrano became hostile to the media and attempted to quash freedom of expression. His business dealings made him confront the business sector. He made everyone uncomfortable and challenged every segment of society, to the point he even started having problems with the very politicians who supported him.

Serrano conducted illegal dealings with electrical companies, an area of millionaire interests. In exchange for their votes on bills regulating the sector, Congressmen blackmailed him and asked for huge sums. In desperation, he attempted a *coup d'etat* from the presidency to abolish Congress and the Supreme Court, the two institutions that stood in the way of his corrupt business dealings.

These problems were compounded by the mayoral elections held halfway into his term in the summer of 1993 because the results did not favor him. This was rare since municipal elections in Guatemala are usually won by the party in power. Voters actually believe it's easier for their local government to deal with the power center if both are led by people under the same party.

Everyone knew Serrano's popularity was hitting bottom. The Christian Democrats held up well and Serrano's party failed to win even one of the important cities. No one could figure this out since Serrano himself was convinced he had people's support. Perhaps there were still some who applauded him and thought he has popular. Had he shown an honest attitude, his order to dissolve Congress might have gained some support. But he was not well intended. He was simply one of those who thought the Constitution could be bypassed, perhaps encouraged by the example of Alberto Fujimori in Peru.

On May 25th, approximately at 4 a.m., we woke amid a tense atmosphere, as in an earthquake. We had experienced an earthquake on February 4, 1976, and before it hit we had felt an eerie chill, a tremor that reached us in a fraction of a second. We felt a similar omen that morning, brought about partly by the howling and barking of dogs.

When I woke up it was totally dark. One of my sons told me, "Look, Dad, we are surrounded. The house is surrounded." We didn't know what to do. A member of my security escort confirmed we were actually surrounded by the police. I met with the whole family to discuss the situation. We turned all the lights on, and made sure the telephones were working. Friends began to call. We asked some reporters to come to our house. It was difficult to find anybody at that hour, about 5 a.m.

We tried to find out what was going on. It took about an hour to get through to the Defense Minister. Meanwhile, I tried to gather as many people as possible to witness that I was being surrounded by police, probably with the intention to arrest me, enter my house, etc. I called colleagues at the Human Rights Commission. By 6:30 a.m. we knew what was happening and, in order to buy some time, I invented a strategy. First, I told the chief of security to call a couple of persons whose names President Serrano had given me. I told him I had just talked to the President and he had told me there was confusion. This probably saved my life and avoided a greater disaster. We turned on the radio and all stations had joined in network, which is the normal way crises are handled in Guatemala.

At 7 a.m. it was clear we were under a *coup d'etat*. I decided to call the Interior Minister at home and his wife answered the phone. She said her husband had not slept at home. So I asked one of my bodyguards to go out and ask the officer in charge of the police operation to come into the house unarmed for a conversation with me.

When the officer arrived we talked in my library. I asked him why he surrounded my house, and he responded he received orders to give me protection. I immediately told him, "Well, stop this protection right away. I am the Human Rights Commissioner." The man insisted he had orders and I insisted it wasn't true because I had talked with President Serrano and he hadn't mentioned it. The officer said, "Wait here. I'll ask confirmation by radio. I know it will be confirmed, so you have a few minutes to do whatever you wish." When he got to the door, he turned around. "I know the order will be confirmed and I'll be told to arrest you."

Q: *Did you use those few minutes to escape?*

RDLC: Exactly. We didn't know at that time the nature of the coup. Whether it was a military coup or where it came from. I left through the neighbor's backyard at the very moment the police were entering the house over the wall to prevent us from fleeing. I beat them by a fraction of a second. A friend was waiting at a neighbor's house and we took off while the officers were sealing the block.

I took my cellular phone with me. Modern technology comes in very handy when you're dealing with *coups d'etat.* I called some friends from the highway and found a house where I could stay. It was the residence of a friend, a politician who lived two blocks away from the National Palace, where the coup had taken place.

Q: *Meaning you became the neighbor of those who perpetrated the coup?*

RDLC: What better place? Who would suspect I would be hiding in the same block where the coup was organized? Once I moved into the house I turned on the television and, at last, learned what it was all about. I stayed at that house making calls until a friend took me to the newspaper *Prensa*

Libre, the most important daily in Guatemala.

There I made a statement that had much impact because I went beyond my functions as Human Rights Commissioner. As ex member of the Constitutional Assembly I assumed the role of constitutionalist and acted to remove legitimacy from the coup. I maintained that constitutional legality could not be interrupted by anyone's orders.

From the newspaper I moved to another house to avoid arrest. Other officials holding important offices had been arrested. In my new hideout I watched on television the ambassadors from the European Union arriving at my house to know about me. I could see the police had contradictory orders. Some were after me; others weren't. It was good to know my wife had finally left the house with the children and had moved in with various relatives.

After confirming that my family was safe, and knowing exactly what the coup was all about, I came out of hiding and called a press conference to address two issues: one, the human rights violation implicit in the action; the other, the violation of the Constitution. I warned we were on the verge of a dictatorship. I also gave a full account of how I fled the police. This made President Serrano furious because the police had been ridiculed, surrounding my house while I was calling a press conference elsewhere.

I made it clear I had no intention of going into clandestinity so as not to legitimize the coup. This gave me a strong leadership. The press conference had been watched in all Guatemala before the newscast was ordered closed and the nation began to live moments of terror. The press had never been subjected to so much harassment and violent actions. Not even under dictatorships.

Serrano committed all kinds of abuse against the media. He ordered all copies of *Crónica* magazine retired from circulation. The same with *La Hora*, which had already hit the streets. The President acted like a real despot.

I showed up at my office at the Human Rights Commission, but I did keep my family in the underground to protect them. The European ambassadors gave me much support. On the fourth day I rejoined my wife and we decided to return to our own house after sending the children to the United States with one of my sisters. I again called a press conference at the headquarters of the Human Rights Commission, in which I announced I was resigning after it had become impossible to protect the population in a situation of unconstitutionality, of illegitimacy. I added that administrative support would continue for all those who requested it, but only in exceptional situations. I thus left the office with the only intention to join the civic movement, the national protest building up against the coup.

Q: *Was it a widespread protest?*

RDLC: Yes, very strong. An anti-coup movement was organized and I was asked to be its vice-president. One of our first activities was a march of thousands following our flag all the way to the presidential palace. There I made a speech appealing to the Constitution and asking for the resignation of President Serrano. Meanwhile, statements opposing the coup started to flow from throughout the country. It soon became clear Serrano had no support whatsoever. This was impressive. It showed Guatemalans had learned a lesson from history. Here we were exercising democracy and defending our institutions. It touched me that my country was all of a sudden in love with democracy. That was new.

It brought to mind the words of Baron of Montesquieu, who said that to defend democracy — just like one would do with wife and kids and any other precious good — one had to get to know it first and love it. How was Guatemala to defend democracy when it didn't know it? People's new behavior came to show they were beginning to know democracy. Once we knew it and loved it, we took to the streets in unison with all segments of society to defend democracy.

After a few days, the perpetrators of the coup began to disintegrate. Once he realized he had problems, President Serrano attempted a new path even more dangerous. He tried to correct the situation through illegal means and called upon corrupt Congressmen, who at that point were ready to accept anything so long as they returned to their status quo in Congress.

Q: *Didn't the President lock himself up with the Congressmen to negotiate a settlement?*

RDLC: Yes, and many were ready to find some accommodation because the civic moment kept growing. Lawyers, businessmen and popular sectors joined the demonstrations against the coup. It was then the Defense Minister called me to his office together with others, including ex President Vinicio Cerezo, to consult us on the constitutional legality of the coup. The minister had not mentioned this meeting to Serrano, who learned what was happening when it was too late. He knew then he was lost. Shortly afterward, the Constitutional Court ruled that Serrano's actions were illegal and he fled to exile.

Q: *Didn't you all try to keep Serrano from fleeing? Why is he allowed to leave the country so easily?*

RDLC: They made it easy for him. They put him on a plane and flew him out of the country. At that moment, they probably wanted to avoid violence and other problems. Their reasoning was that with Serrano out of the way things were easier to resolve. This was the logic of the Defense Minister, who is the one who lets him get away. Serrano was a criminal, a man who had committed serious crimes. Yet he was permitted to flee. Those who helped him escape later said they should have indicted him and forced him to return the money he stole.

After this outcome I returned to the headquarters of the Human Rights Commission and issued a public communiqué explaining Serrano had violated human rights and pointing out his responsibility. This coincided with the ruling of the Constitutional Court, which also dismissed the vice-president for trying to assume the presidency in connivance with Serrano, and ordered Congress to elect a new president.

The Guatemalan Guerrillas

By Santiago Aroca

Four Guatemalan guerrilla organizations have waged the longest civil war in Latin America. The Guerrilla Army of the Poor (*Ejército Guerrillero de los Pobres, EGP*), the Revolutionary Organization of People in Arms (*Organización Revolucionaria del Pueblo en Armas, ORPA*), the Rebel Armed Forces (*Fuerzas Armadas Rebeldes, FAR*), and the Guatemalan Labor Party (*Partido Guatemalteco del Trabajo, PGT*) are now integrated under the name of National Revolutionary Unity of Guatemala (*Unidad Revolucionaria Nacional de Guatemala, URNG*).

URNG is negotiating with the Guatemalan government to end a war that began in 1961. The United Nations and various European governments, as well as Mexico, have mediated at the different stages of the dialogue seeking a peaceful solution.

Ironically, the group demonstrating the strongest commitment to the peace process is the one that started the violence — PGT, a communist organization with strong ties to Cuba. At its helm is Rodrigo Asturias, alias *Comandante Gaspar Ilom,* the son of Miguel Angel Asturias, a world known Guatemalan writer and winner of the 1967 Nobel Prize for Literature.

The most violent organization is ORPA, which in the 70s claimed responsibility for the murder of U.S. Ambassador John Gordon Mein. ORPA is the group more reluctant to reach a peace agreement.

EGP is the organization with the largest structure. Its center of operations is located in the Department of Quiché, where it began fighting in 1972, after one of its armed units crossed the border from Mexico. At that time the Guatemalan army had a limited presence in the area. In 1975 these guerrillas executed José Luis Arenas in front of his employees. Arenas, one of the largest landowners, owned the farm La Perla in Chajul.

The Guatemalan army responded attacking guerrilla positions. But by the end of 1978, EGP was capable not only of holding its ground but of taking entire villages, where they held public meetings and destroyed jails that kept Indians prisoners.

In 1982, Gen. Efraín Ríos Montt, who reached the Guatemalan presidency by a military coup, changed army tactics dramatically. He organized civilian patrols to guarantee the people's loyalty. The immediate reaction in many communities was to withdraw and shun contact with the guerrillas. This allowed the regular army to inflict heavy blows to the rebels who in turn responded with extreme cruelty, executing the members of captured patrols.

The year 1995 was a year of severe weakness among the guerrillas, although they were still capable of gathering hundreds of combatants to ambush military units. More and more the guerrillas resembled mere terrorist groups, despite the fact that the cause for their struggle — the lack of land for poor peasants — remained unresolved.

7

Mr. President

Question: *Why did Congress end up electing you president?*
Ramiro de León Carpio: My performance in the Constitutional Assembly, my political activities, and my professional achievements had brought me popular recognition. But there's no doubt that my performance as Human Rights Commissioner had earned me the most extraordinary sympathy.

I remember in January of 1993 the Guatemalan daily *Prensa Libre* inaugurated a new section in the paper to highlight the Man of the Year, an outstanding person in Guatemala who deserved recognition for his accomplishments, actions and attitudes in favor of the nation. I had the honor to be the first selected.

It gave me great satisfaction and underlined the leadership I had exerted, my activism and presence in the national arena. In those days I could visit the remotest of places, including the most isolated indigenous communities, and people recognized me. The first time I had gone on a tour with my cousin Jorge Carpio we traveled to the Quiché Department on a Sunday and we visited the market, went to mass, and walked around every place. There were big crowds of Maya Indians dressed in their typical embroidered colorful garments. Jorge commented how people who passed before us never bothered to turn their heads to notice. The day they recognize us, said Jorge, the day we are greeted by the indigenous community, we will have accomplished the penetration we need. We both experienced this recognition afterward. Through his electoral activities, Jorge attained tremendous penetration. I got it through my trips to save human lives, families leaving their communities or returning to them on account of the war.

I was called once to aid a family who wanted to return to its community. This was an area of heavy battle, so I prepared myself for the worst. On our way there we ran into highway patrols. One officer approached me and offered troops to escort and protect me. When we arrived at the village, many Indians had come out with clubs and hatchets. One of them blew a huge bull's horn to call on others to come out. The soldiers feared the situation would get out of hand and had grenades ready just in case. The clubs intimidated me, but the crowd was receptive to my speech and calmed down. "I was impressed by your speech," the officer later told me.

People talked to me afterward. I explained what their rights were. Each one would then tell me his or her story. A woman with three small children, for example, told me the guerrillas had killed her husband. That was why, she said, she helped the civilian patrols who fought the guerrillas. A young man told me he had been a guerrilla fighter until he felt deceived. Now he wanted to defend his country. And so on. I listened attentively and could tell no one had ever taken these people seriously. I understood how important the self-defense civilian patrols were to them and how much harm the guerrillas had inflicted on these communities. The foreign media have given hardly any space to these issues in their newspaper editions abroad.

On another occasion I was caught in heavy guerrilla fire. I traveled to a village as Human Rights Commissioner accompanying the Defense Minister. When our helicopters arrived we were received by artillery fire. We had to jump and run into trenches, where we waited four or five hours listening to the whistling of bullets over our heads. This experience helped me understand the reality of the Guatemalan war. People in the cities didn't know there was a war. They were hardly aware that while their lives continued someone was under attack or finding death by a terrorist artifact. The people who suffered the most were the Indians and the peasants, the humblest and the poorest.

When the news of our dangerous incident in the trenches ran on television, friends called me to warn me that maybe it had all been orchestrated by the army. I simply replied the bullets were real and I had seen soldiers fall when they were wounded. The army invited me to these dangerous areas, but not to mount fake attacks. They did it to show me the conditions in which that war was fought. They lived in the mud, with low-quality shoes, without adequate equipment. In those risky positions soldiers were relieved every six months and it was dangerous to get them out. The guerrillas attacked even more ferociously during those relief operations.

These trips gave me a more integral formation as a leader. They strengthened my objectivity and sense of fairness. Defense Minister Gen. Mario Enríquez invited me once to a farewell ceremony of soldiers who had completed 30 years of military service. Had I not seen it with my own eyes I would have never believed it. The soldiers — all of them peasants, Indians — cried their hearts out when they left. While the music played they kept crying, crying, crying.

Q: *Tell us about the presidential nomination process.*

RDLC: The Constitutional Court had ruled the measures taken by President Serrano illegal. Serrano was out of the country. The vice president was forced to resign and Congress met to elect a new president.

While all these things developed I remained at home. One Friday I came home from work and found a bunch of visitors waiting for me. They stayed until the early hours of Saturday. Jorge Arenas, a friend, commented that my name was being mentioned in Congress halls as possible president. Jorge Arenas had replaced me as deputy general secretary of UCN when I left the party, and had gone through similar pain. He had characterized himself as a solid mediator, a man who could handle political dialogue and negotiation with any individual or group.

Friends and all kinds of people kept parading through my house to tell me that the climate in Congress was favorable to my nomination and that there was no other public figure in the country who could be better chosen to rescue Guatemalan democracy. There were also groups opposing my nomination who circulated rumors that I had been offered the job and had turned it down. This was perhaps the factor that prompted me to authorize my official nomination. I took it as a challenge. I felt I had a mission, all the while knowing it was to be an extremely difficult one. Some well-intentioned political analysts made the point that if I wanted to be president I could always wait for the next election. Yet electoral activity turned me off. I didn't want to be a conditional president. It was preferable to face a more adverse challenge, one not compromised by businessmen, the military or political parties.

On his own initiative Jorge Arenas talked to different political representations in Congress. But the most influential factor was a spontaneous, massive popular demonstration where, displaying banners, people demanded at the top of their voices that I be elected. No one organized it; it was totally spontaneous. At that moment the business sector did not oppose nor support my nomination. It was to their benefit , of course, if the person elected was not likely to create problems for them or oppose their interests. They feared the Human Rights Commissioner's unsettling message about economic and social rights. And political parties felt pretty much the same way. So I really can't understand how I became president. The three power factors — the military, the business sector and the politicians — did not support me. I was still the Human Rights Commissioner and, though my relations with progressive members of the military was good, it was obvious they wouldn't want me as president. The whole process remains an inexplicable mystery, whose only explanation could perhaps lie on Jorge Arenas's mediating abilities and the many friends I had in and out of Congress.

I participated only at the end of the process when Congress called to inform me there was parliamentary agreement, but that the Defense Minister did not accept me. Right there and then I felt compelled to go for it. I am a stubborn person. When I am told I can't do something, my whole system works up to doing it. Analysts have pointed out that I am a man of turbulent currents who performs better in moments of crisis than in moments of calmness. They even exaggerate to say that when things are calm with me I invent a problem. What I accepted with the presidency was the opportunity to be at the helm of a ship sailing under a storm, and to pilot it, if not to a safe port, at least out of the tempest. That I have accomplished. The ship is now out of the storm, still moving but in tranquil waters, heading to safe port.

I called the Defense Minister and asked him point blank if it was true he opposed my nomination for president. I then refreshed his memory about Serrano's crisis and how I had told him in his office that the President was violating the Constitution. I also talked with other eight Cabinet members and mentioned the military's opposition to my nomination. Their response was the military would not have it their way. A representation of army officers visited me at my house and assured me they would accept Congress's decision.

I immediately called my friends to tell them the military obstacle was out of the way. Gathered at my house over coffee, they made lists of possible opponents and supporters.

They tried to find a vice president and some of the names they mentioned were really dangerous.

Q: *Didn't the Christian Democrats offer nominating you as their presidential candidate in the next election if you withdrew your name at that moment?*

RDLC: They did mention that possibility. But that was a scenario I never considered because of my disappointment with partisan politics.

Finally a group of businessmen came to visit me at my house. I talked about my values, my ideas, my approach to politics and the maturity I had reached throughout the years. I told them I felt ready to lead the nation in a democratic way, though conscious of the limitations imposed by national and international reality. In a few words I tried to gain their confidence and asked them to support me if I was elected. There was no rejection on their part.

Summing up, the business sector was not going to influence the process, the military removed their obstacle, and among the politicians I only had the opposition of my cousin Jorge Carpio, who was honest enough to express it publicly. He basically opposed me because, as a relative of mine, the Constitution precluded him to run for president in a future election.

When the nomination was voted in Congress I won, though not by absolute majority. I had a strong lead over my closest contender, Arturo Herbruger Asturias. After he, in a display of the decency and honesty that have characterized him all his life, withdrew his name from the ballot, I was elected unanimously. This is how I became president.

Q: *How does it feel having been elected by a Congress with so many discredited and corrupted members?*

RDLC: I thought about this a lot. Shortly before the vote some Congressmen asked me for an amnesty. I said no. I imagine they also asked the other candidate and were rejected or they would have voted for him. Even after I was elected they asked me to include some reference to pardoning in my acceptance speech. I replied that my speech would make reference to corruption. Indeed, my piece enumerated the steps I planned to take against corruption, beginning with the abolishment of the President's confidential millionaire funds. Even Congressmen applauded this as something unprecedented in the history of Guatemala.

Confidential funds were traditionally used by presidents for all kinds of corruption and acts of power abuse. They have used these millionaire funds for everything. In his last year in power, Serrano had access to approximately 150 millions of quetzals (approximately $37.5 million) without having to explain one penny. His predecessors, with some honorable exceptions, did exactly the same.

Of course I also thought of what to do with Congress, an institution controlled by a corrupt group. It was ironic to have been elected by a group repudiated by Guatemalan society. Yet they had elected me on behalf of the people, and at that moment I was the person with the quality and characteristics needed to rescue the institutional order and move the country forward. Besides, it was a consensual mandate from the civilian segments of society, from labor unions to the private sector.

I don't believe there has been another president in our history who took office under the conditions I did — with no staff and no government program; amid an acute institutional, political, economic and social crisis; finances in a shambles with high debt; and great expectations placed on me to resolve it all.

Yet I accepted the presidency as one more challenge — perhaps the greatest, the riskiest and the most important challenge in my life. It demanded a big sacrifice from me, my wife, my children, the entire family. But it has been worth it; I have no regrets.

Q: *How can a president function in an atmosphere of generalized mistrust and without the support of a political party?*

RDLC: In one of my first speeches, given in the 1993 Ibero-American Presidents' Summit in Salvador de Bahía, Brazil, shortly after taking office, I said Guatemala was a country of significant contrasts and paradoxes: a nation with many illiterate and yet a Nobel Prize in Literature, Miguel Angel Asturias; a nation with no peace and yet a Nobel Peace Prize, Rigoberta Menchú; a nation with a long tradition of human rights violations and yet a Human Rights Commissioner as its president.

Yes, I arrived at the presidency under special conditions. The fact that I had no political party made it difficult. For instance, the morning after the election I woke up as a president who had no one working for him. There were of course officials doing their jobs, but none had been placed there by me with so many problems out there. We had inherited problems such as strikes, students burning buses, etc. And there was, fundamentally, political and institutional instability. The corrupt wing of Congress saw me as their enemy from Day One. They kept pushing for an unconstitutional stroke on my part, which differently from Serrano I could have launched with impunity with the kind of support I enjoyed. Yet I opted for the legal, longest path.

My first confrontation was thus with politicians while the business sector watched in wonder. To govern in those conditions was difficult, and the population must have understood the situation, for early in 1995 my popularity rating exceeded the numbers at the time of election. After 19 months in power, more people actually supported me, a totally new phenomenum in this country. In 1995 I reached 81 percent of acceptance, in contrast to 76 percent when I became president. I guess people knew the country was in real bad shape when I took over. I want to forget my first six months in power, the longest days of my life. My schedule ran seven days a week with 20-hour journeys.

The advantage of reaching power alone, without political links, is that you don't have to compromise or make deals with anybody, like my predecessors had to do. President Julio César Méndez Montenegro, for example, is one of the few civilians who have reached the presidency. He came with the Revolutionary Party dating back to 1944, although with a different ideology. To take office he had to make a deal with the military. My only deal was with the Guatemalan people.

Q: *Did you remove the Defense Minister and the Military Chief of Staffs immediately after becoming president?*

RDLC: In 22 days I dismissed two Defense Ministers and one Presidential Chief of Staff, all high-ranking generals. I decapitated the high-command of the army.

Q: *Why did you feel the need to do that?*

RDLC: The historical moment called for a change of guard. The nation needed officers with a more progressive mentality and behavior, more in agreement with the national circumstance and closer to peace and democracy. The higher positions had to be filled by officers committed to the role of the army within a democratic system.

Q: *But what were the specific reasons given for the dismissals?*

RDLC: For months I devoted a lot of time to penetrate the military. I studied, investigated, analyzed. I listened to the advice of officers whom I considered the new generation of the military — people with a clear, progressive mind, conscious of the democratic reality of the nation.

One of the dismissals involved the cousin of the Defense Minister, an officer who played an important role in Serrano's coup. The second was a similar case. I also made changes at other levels to boost military stability and national institutional standing. Never before had such decisions been made in this country by the President as Commander in Chief of the Armed Forces.

I traveled extensively throughout the country to make direct contact with the people. I wanted to exert a new governing style, leaving the presidential palace and hitting the road. Among other tasks accomplished in these trips, I delivered the Constitutional 8-percent fund to the 330 municipalities. This I completed exactly two months after taking office. I talked to the mayors and handed them the money in public ceremonies to force them to explain how they planned to invest it. This resulted in a positive contact with the population. What I like the most is when people of all ages come to me and tell me, "We are praying for you, Mr. President. God bless you."

Not many presidents had traveled to the countryside after taking office. As candidates they toured the country campaigning for the first vote and the runoff. Once elected, they locked themselves up in the palace, tired of tours and speeches. Since I had not gone through an electoral campaign, I reached office fresh and eager to go on the road. Direct contact with people has helped me prioritize their needs and respond to them with concrete deeds.

8

On The Trail of Death

Question: *What specific goals did you set for your administration in the early days?*

Ramiro de León Carpio: My government program had five points. First, the consolidation of democracy and the state of law by advancing the modernization of political institutions to increase people's participation. Second, the fight against poverty, which was the fundamental challenge of the moment. Third, the transformation of our industrial production to conform our economy to international conditions. Fourth, the conservation of the environment and the rational use of our renewable natural resources. And finally, the fifth point addressed institutional modernization. In other words, the basic goals of our reforms aimed at improving the general performance of government so as not to allow inefficiency neutralize society.

Under those five points my program — which was to cover the remaining six-month period of 1993 and the years 1994 and 1995 — addressed the financial aspects of the economic crisis I found.

Q: *Let's return to a difficult topic. You assumed the presidency after years defending human rights in obvious confrontation with the military. What happened to the officers you had accused of human rights abuse? What did you do with them?*

RDLC: Human rights abuse is no longer a government or presidential policy in Guatemala. Of course, there are still problems. When I assumed the presidency the armed confrontation between the army and the guerrillas was still the primary source of human rights violations. But the change was the expressed effort by the President to stop the abuse.

Indeed, my background as human rights champion generated a special circumstance, both flattering and controversial. There was a lot of expectation from my presidency. People expected changes. They commented that at last the nation was led by an honest man, a man of courage who fought for people's individual and social rights. They expected that in two months the situation would be corrected, particularly in relation to human rights.

My problem is that my presidency is always compared to my discourse and attitude during my days as Human Rights Commissioner. You see, I have gone full circle from writing about human rights, defending them as commissioner, and finally enforcing them as President, which is the most difficult stage. For this I had to set a strategy and make this issue the principal objective of my term. My ultimate concern is to reach the end of my mandate with an absolute respect toward individual human rights as a result of the end of the armed confrontation and the signing of a peace treaty.

Q: *The so-called self-defense civilian patrols have been frequently accused of arbitrary and violent conduct. Do you support them?*

RDLC: I said it as Human Rights Commissioner and now as President. The self-defense civilian patrols emerged as a strategic military necessity to curb the guerrillas' advance. We signed an agreement with the guerrillas to stop creating patrols unless it becomes absolutely necessary. In other words, the guerrillas ended up also accepting the patrols. In many places I have ordered the patrols dissolved. They remain only in those areas where there's still combat and confrontation, or that guerrillas use as passages.

As far as compulsory military service, I suspended it until a law regulating it is approved. The Constitution establishes it as a right as well as a patriotic duty. The new law will regulate it to avoid discrimination, forced and violent drafting, and recruiting minors under 18. Military service should combine military and social duties.

My presidency has had some isolated though important problems. One of them was the death of my cousin Jorge Carpio shortly after I took office. And others, such as the death of Epaminondas González, President of the Constitutional Court, and the death of a university student after an unfortunate police intervention in San Carlos university. These are unfortunate events that also occur in other countries. The difference is that here we don't have an agile judicial system to clear the cases rapidly. Here the truth takes long to come about, if ever.

Q: *Why do you say justice is not efficient?*

RDLC: The murder of Jorge Carpio is in the hands of a judicial court. My administration did everything within its means. We presented one of the weapons used in the crime. There is a suspect under custody charged with the crime. All patrol members charged were arrested, though most of them were later released by the judicial system. This is a case that, unfortunately, has not been cleared.

The Interior Ministry and the police were severely criticized for two regrettable police interventions — a raid in San Carlos university, where one student was killed amid the effort to control students throwing rocks and burning urban buses, and an eviction authorized by a judge of the farm La Estancia. Responding to a resolution issued by the new Human Rights Commissioner, the Interior Minister and other officials were dismissed. Furthermore, a committee headed by the Human Rights Commissioner is investigating the case of San Carlos university.

The case of Jorge Carpio is particularly painful to me. Hardly a month after my taking office a gang of assailants blocked his car and killed him and two other people accompanying him apparently with the intention to rob him. This took place at night in a solitary place, on a highway known for many incidents of assault and robbery. Before he left, Jorge had been advised not to take this road.

When the crime occurred I had a good relation with him. After I resigned from UCN there followed a period of cold distance, but after a while I began recovering the relationship. Jorge Arenas invited me to a few meetings with my cousin and our cordial mutual affection was revived. There were no problems when I took office, not even after Jorge publicly announced he would not support my candidacy. I remember that shortly after I became president we met at my house. He had come with his son Rodrigo.

Q: *Didn't that conversation turn out to be bitter?*

RDLC: For him, yes. Yet that fact did not keep us from having a cordial, lively talk. He confessed it had been hard for him to acknowledge that I had achieved what he had failed to accomplish for other reasons. And he congratulated me while we discussed the future, the difficult situation ahead.

Jorge died on a Saturday. The previous Thursday he had come to lunch with me at the presidential residence. Again we had a pleasant conversation, discussing various national issues and problems. He told me of his plans to travel through the country. He was a hard-working man, devoting much of his time to the party. He was going on tour knowing he could never be a presidential candidate because he was my cousin and the Constitution banned relatives of prior presidents to run. Two days later he was killed. I cried. It was a horrible crime and, as a citizen, I will never cease to protest and demand clarification and justice.

Q: *However, his widow and daughter complain that you haven't done all within your power to clear this crime. They have launched an intense campaign demanding clarification. What do you think* *of their campaign?*

RDLC: I have learned about it with pain. They know that no one is more interested in clarifying Jorge's murder than I am, for sentimental and political reasons, because of my affection toward him. I am committed to have his death cleared. To me it's a matter of great responsibility. Judicial incompetence, however, especially in the prior Supreme Court, has hindered progress in the investigation. We gave them all they needed. We delivered the weapon with which he was killed. In any other country that would have been sufficient evidence to arrest, try and punish the culprits. I even obtained ballistic cooperation from the U.S. Federal Bureau of Investigation (FBI) and Mexico.

The campaign by Jorge's widow and daughter gives me pain and sorrow. There has been political manipulation. The purpose of the fabricated scenario is to gain partisan political advantage, but it has not worked out for the interests behind it. Most Guatemalans do not believe it. It's useless to try at all costs to depict as political a crime surrounded by elements that clearly indicate it was not political. People at UCN consider — and I know this from friends who are members — that it's preferable to have Jorge Carpio dead at the hands of the military, even if no one believes this version, than by a bunch of criminal assailants on a dangerous road in the middle of the night.

Q: *There's another case that has had a lot of exposure. I'm referring to guerrilla leader Efraín Bámaca, whose wife, an American lawyer, has staged hunger strikes in Guatemala and Washington demanding clarification of her husband's death. What is your opinion on the Bámaca case?*

RDLC: This is a case I know well from the time I was Human Rights Commissioner. In 1992 I received a report through Francisco Villagrán, spokesman of the National Revolutionary Unity of Guatemala (URNG), the umbrella organization that groups all guerrilla organizations. It was about the disappearance of this guerrilla leader, who had a record of 17 years of involvement in all types of terrorist and subversive activity. I investigated the case and came up with various scenarios. One of them had guerrilla commander Bámaca dying in combat. Another one had him committing suicide on the verge of getting arrested. One way or the other I concluded Bámaca was dead. This was in 1992 and I handled the case as Human Rights Commissioner, not as President. I based my conclusions on the URNG's information about Bámaca, whose war name was *Comandante Everardo*. His body was never found, however, just as thousands of other bodies from both sides were never found. Guerrillas usually picked up their dead and buried them. Very rarely did guerrilla bodies remain on the battlefield. Who knows then where all these bodies are buried?

When had Bámaca died? No one knew. The accusation was that he was alive, held in a clandestine prison, and subjected to tortures. The legal mechanisms, however, have proved otherwise. Even Mrs. Jennifer Harbury, Bámaca's wife, has conceded his death. My responsibility is therefore safe in the sense that he is not illegally held.

Q: *But was he ever detained? Did the military have him under custody?*

RDLC: My conclusion as commissioner was that he had died. The exact circumstances are difficult to tell. Although the body was never found, as a magistrate of conscience I concluded he was dead, basing my conclusion on all the elements given me and the investigations I performed. It is therefore totally false that Bámaca was ever held in a clandestine prison. I can attest to the fact that in my government there has never been a clandestine prison.

Every possible procedure has been used to find Bámaca's body. The nation's Attorney General carried out all the investigations, the Supreme Court intervened, and so did the new Human Rights Commissioner and all the pertinent institutions. The results of investigations point to Bámaca's death, which is unfortunate but understandable, considering he was a guerrilla fighter active in the civil war for 17 years. The logical and normal outcome for him was not to have died in bed, but in combat.

There has been an intense publicity campaign surrounding the Bámaca case, including a movie project and a book to be written by his alleged wife, American lawyer Jennifer Harbury. She has traveled to Guatemala frequently and has received full official assistance in her trips. She staged a public demonstration, a hunger strike before the Government Palace, and was never bothered. Her rights and integrity were fully respected. Since she insisted her husband was alive, she was asked to prove in court her accusation that we were holding him in a clandestine prison. Of course, Mrs. Harbury has not to this day proved her accusations nor presented any evidence to substantiate her allegations. Which leads me to believe that her claim eventually will be dismissed due to lack of substance.

I must admit Mrs. Harbury caused tremendous harm to Guatemala's image, particularly in the United States where it was widely reported that we had her husband under custody. Her marriage to Bámaca, by the way, has never been reasonably proved. In Guatemala Bámaca's parents denied it. He was apparently linked to someone else. But, in all, circumstances indicate there was a clear desire to harm Guatemala, and Mrs. Harbury did precisely that with all the publicity the case obtained in the United States.

Q: *What was the impact in Guatemala, and how did you react to the spectacular hunger strike taking place right in front of the Government Palace, exactly the place from where you exercised the nation's presidency?*

RDLC: It caused a negative impression inside Guatemala. Even the media demanded her expulsion, according to polls which also showed that people wanted her deported and her visas to enter our country denied. People were upset because here was this American lady doing all these things to hurt Guatemala.

This was a case of a guerrilla commander who in all likelihood took many lives before giving his own. He worked with the urban guerrillas placing explosive artifacts in terrorist actions, probably killing children, women, elderly people. He was a full-fledged guerrilla fighter, someone who may have killed not only army officers and soldiers, but many innocent people who had no part in the war.

I have no doubt that the URNG is behind the Bámaca case. Not only is there a propaganda angle to this affair, but also an economic interest. After the first book is published there will be a sequel, and even a movie will be filmed to bring more money to the story.

Q: *What did you do when coming to work every morning you ran into Mrs. Harbury on a hunger strike at the door of your workplace? It must have been unpleasant.*

RDLC: A few years ago nobody was allowed to protest before the Government Palace. Since I became President I took the appropriate measures to allow anyone wishing to protest to do so in front of the palace. Today the Constitution Square is used by union leaders and the homeless to demonstrate. I have often abandoned my office to go down and talk to homeless people. It's a free, democratic mechanism that did not exist before. It does today. Today they come and yell at the President, carry banners, and say whatever they wish. When Mrs. Harbury announced her hunger strike I worried about her health and asked that she be taken care of as well as possible. I even ordered that if she incurred in health problems that she be taken to the Guatemalan Red Cross, always looking after her good health.

Of course, her decision to go on hunger strike was respected, as was her right to protest peacefully. I simply endured the propagandistic pressure resulting from her actions.

Q: *What actions have you taken lately on the Bámaca case, the death of American citizen Michael DeVine, and the accusations of CIA involvement in Guatemala?*

RDLC: In spite of the various versions of the disappearance or death of Efraín Bámaca in 1992, and because it is a typical case resulting from the domestic armed confrontation, the Guatemalan government considers it has taken every judicial action to thoroughly investigate the case. Therefore, in accordance with the spirit of the agreement that established a committee for the historic clarification of human rights violations and violent acts linked to the armed conflict, the case must be transferred to the jurisdiction of that committee created under peace negotiations. My government deems inappropriate to promote investigations and judicial processes of cases linked to the armed confrontation. To do so would only harm the peace process and would foster polarization and political manipulation.

Regarding the case of American citizen Michael DeVine, whose death occurred in 1990, the Guatemalan government took the corresponding legal actions that led to penal sentences against members of the military: 30-year sentences to five soldiers; a 20-year sentence to Capt. Hugo Contreras, who unfortunately escaped from prison in May 1993.

Q: *Two Guatemalan officers are being pointed out abroad as allegedly responsible for this crime — Cols. Julio Roberto Alpírez and Mario García Catalán. What actions have you taken against them?*

RDLC: My government, through its Public Ministry, reopened the investigation of this case and will continue its efforts to enforce justice at any level. To facilitate this I temporarily suspended both officers from their functions to allow the judicial process to freely rule against them if it so determines. This is unprecedented in the history of Guatemala. Furthermore, my government intensified the search of Capt. Hugo Contreras, and has requested Interpol's cooperation abroad. Among other things, his picture was posted on bulletin boards and circulated in the national press, and a reward of 100,000 quetzals (approximately $25,000) was offered for information leading to his capture.

As far as the CIA involvement in Guatemala, there are multiple international treaties regulating relations among nations on security issues, validating communication and exchange among their various intelligence institutions. There are programs establishing bilateral and multilateral efforts against drug-trafficking, money laundering, illegal immigration, international terrorism, arms contraband and ecological depredation.

About the alleged illegal association between the CIA and Col. Alpírez, the military is carrying out an internal investigation, and the Public Ministry is also conducting the corresponding judicial procedure. The Guatemalan government has requested and will appreciate any information the United States could offer on this issue.

Q: *How did you feel when in 1994 the U.S. State Department issued a critical report about human rights in Guatemala?*

RDLC: The report also had positive aspects, but the media only highlighted the negative. It spoke well of the efforts and accomplishments of our government. There were two ways of interpreting the report. One was to view it as an update of an existing situation not yet resolved, for which the current government was not responsible. Another way was as an accusation against my government for not taking appropriate measures. Of course, we would all want the culprits to go to jail and pay for their crimes, but it's not that simple when the judicial structure is deficient or, in certain cases, corrupt.

I accept the second reading making me responsible for not yet accomplishing complete and total respect of human rights. I take it as constructive criticism. It's true that there's still a lot to do and I am devoting my best efforts to this issue. People must understand it's not easy to go from the barbaric to paradise. We are on the right track, a lot better than a few years ago, though not yet where we wish to be.

When I was the commissioner I was independent and critical toward others and myself. I don't see any reason to change now. It all turns around against me today because I have to respect the objectivity and faculties of the current Human Rights Commissioner.

Yes, there have been harsh reports against Guatemala. Not only from the U.S. State Department but also from Dr. Mónica Pinto, the United Nations expert adviser. Both documents criticized us for not having ended human rights violations, while at the same time acknowledged improvements and efforts by the current government. I can only say that they're right, but they must also recognize that today there's no institutional policy of abuse. There's a war going on in Guatemala and, to the best of our ability, we will make every effort to sign a peace agreement to stop all the violence.

With this I am conceding that the culture of lack of respect for human rights and individual dignity under which Guatemalans lived for too long is difficult to overcome. But we are working seriously on this issue, as can be seen from the measures we have taken so far and will be taking during my term, such as the ones mentioned about the cases of Bámaca, DeVine, the CIA connection, etc., as well as the suspension of high-ranking officers and the dissolution of the self-defense civilian patrols and the military commissioners.

Regarding the economic, social or cultural rights included in our Constitution, we have begun a process to respond to these needs, particularly with the rural population. The challenge continues the same as during the past 500 years: to improve health care, education, nutrition and the environment. We need to reach out especially to the population suffering extreme poverty, and to those more vulnerable like children and women.

Another topic worth mentioning is freedom of expression. I say with pride that during my administration we have respected the individual right of informing and the collective right of being informed, and the press is the first to recognize it. In other words, Guatemala enjoys a climate of freedom of the press, with only a few isolated exceptions like everywhere else in the world. There's also absolute respect of the journalist's right to have access to the information, an unthinkable practice before, and one of the pillars of the democratic system in place in Guatemala today.

Q: *Sometimes the paradox of the Human Rights Commissioner turned President is explained by saying Guatemala continues under the real power of the military. Is Guatemala experiencing a process of militarization?*

RDLC: I vigorously reject that notion. My government has assumed unprecedented attitudes toward recuperating the space belonging to civilian power, which due to ineptness and problems attributed mostly to the civilian leadership, had been usurped by the military. In reversing the situation, the military has expressly retreated and given up that space in favor of the civilian power.

To speak about militarization is totally inaccurate. No president has enjoyed the freedom I've had to elaborate and implement my political, economic and social programs. I have found no obstacles; all the contrary, I have felt supported on every issue. Even on military issues, on which I have naturally sought the advice of experts as is done in the rest of the world, the final decision has always been the President's, which goes to show that the military yields to civilian power.

In one of my speeches on Army Day I publicly said the President promoted the subordination of the military to civilian power. I wouldn't have had it any other way. Had I not had absolute freedom to act, I would have forsaken the presidency on Day One.

Of course I have had difficult moments. For instance, I had appointed an Interior Minister, an excellent person and a wise, cordial attorney and academician, who lacked control and decision-making skills to guarantee the public safety of our citizens. This was at a time when common crime and violence had increased. Many people approached me and asked me to fire him. The media also took issue with the situation. I finally had to dismiss him. Was it military pressure? Of course not. I just had to dismiss an incompetent official.

It's true that people talk about militarization. But if you read the recent polls, the military is frequently praised. They have become a factor for peace. When students burned buses to protest the fare hike, for example, we sent soldiers out to the streets to restore order. People applauded every time they saw a soldier or an officer. They felt protected. When the transportation strike, which later led to the problems at San

Carlos university, we had to intervene through members of the armed forces who guarded the buses. People just want safety and don't care who provides it. As opposed to issues like inflation and the economy, which only concern certain people, safety issues affect every segment of society. The higher, middle and lower classes. That's why the militarization myth is an exaggeration.

Based on safety arguments I have occasionally been asked publicly to get the military involved. And the Constitution establishes among functions and goals of the military to guarantee order, peace and tranquility for every citizen.

So when I had to dismiss the Interior Minister I replaced him with another civilian and a military deputy. Since I wanted the second person to serve as liaison with the armed forces, I appointed an army officer who had been acting as Director of Intelligence. I admit that such appointment carried the price of being perceived by the international community as a step backward. But it was well received by the domestic community. Besides, it was put to test with good results during the operations carried out in cooperation with the army.

Q: *When you mention that public safety tops the list of concerns in every poll, are you saying that people are still attentive of the guerrilla activities?*

RDLC: No. People don't associate the guerrillas with safety problems. Public safety tops the polls every week, falling to second place sometimes only to the economic situation. However, the internal armed conflict per se takes secondary places in the polls, if only because, alas, people have become accustomed to the guerrillas after so many years. I'm not saying it doesn't affect everyday life. If a bomb explodes one day in an electrical tower, a blackout will occur in some province, and they will be without electricity for a few days while we, with great efforts, restore the tower and bring back power.

Burglary, murder, robbery are worse common crimes that take place in every country. They become a nightmare for any president.

Q: *A high number of gangs operate in Guatemala carrying out kidnaping, burglary, extortion. Who controls these groups?*
RDLC: There is a big social decomposition in Guatemala as a result of poverty and misery. These factors serve as a culture broth. There is no doubt that misery has forced many to commit murder and other crimes. Some are still kids, street kids who reflect the terrible phenomenon of our society. Who raised those children to be what they are? Society itself, the injustice of our rotten society.

Juvenile delinquency is caused by social problems, economic hardship, lack of values. In other words, a series of factors generate this delinquency effect, a high percentage of which is also a consequence of the absence of law enforcement and the lack of prompt judicial procedures. It takes us longer to capture a criminal than for a judge to release him for lack of evidence. Our law enforcement and judicial systems are plagued with inefficiencies.

True, violence can be found everywhere in the world — in Washington, Tampa, Chicago, Madrid, Tokyo, San Salvador. But there's also truth in the old axiom saying that the disease of many is consolation for fools. Guatemalans here point their index finger at me. Little do they care if other cities in the world live in violence and crime.

Violence is a widespread evil, even in countries with resources and effective security systems. Our problem is compounded by our inefficient security, not well equipped, poorly compensated. It's the kind of structural reform we must tackle.

I ask but two actions from my Interior Ministry officials: one is to give back psychological tranquility to our citizens; the other to dismantle the criminal gangs. We need to set the foundation, change the police structure, and create the professional school of law enforcement as a legacy to the next government, so as to provide our future generations with an efficient and effective safety. For all this we need more resources.

In the meantime, the army cooperates occasionally in

safety situations, though that does not mean, as it has been led to believe, that soldiers on the streets reflect the nation's militarization. The army serves as a liaison for dealing with certain law-enforcement operations against organized crime, drug-traffickers, and environment depredators.

Above, with his family: (standing, left to right) Alejandro de León Duque, Luis Edmenguer, Ramiro de León Duque, Gustavo Valle Leoni, and Jorge Eduardo de León Duque. (Seating, left to right) Claudia de Edmenguer with Daniela Edmenguer, Maria Eugenia de De León Carpio with Christian Edmenguer, the President with Melany Edmenguer, Susana de De León with Ana Isabel de León, and Ninethe de Valle with Luis Eduardo Valle. (Right) The President speaks in Guatemala's mountainous countryside.

The unique circumstances in which he reached the presidency — no party, no program, no staff — allowed President De León Carpio to choose collaborators with no agendas. Here he talks with attorney and entrepreneur Jorge Arenas Menes, a skilled, indefatigable negotiator who helped the President defuse various crises throughout his administration.

One of the warmest demonstrations President De León Carpio received from the indigenous communities took place during an event that gathered 10,000 Indians in Todos Santos Cuchumatanes on the second anniversary of his presidential term. Above, he carries a little Indian girl. Right, the President and First Lady María Eugenia salute the crowd wearing typical Indian garments.

President De León Carpio shakes hands with school children greeting him during the inauguration of a primary school.

The President insists on visiting faraway villages never before visited by a Guatemalan president. His good relations with indigenous communities have helped him resolve multiple social problems consistently neglected in the past.

A significant change in the respect for human rights under President De León Carpio's administration has improved the relationship between Guatemala and Washington. Above, chatting with President Bill Clinton in Washington. Right, visiting with French President Jacques Chirac in France, where he sought France's support for the Guatemalan peace process.

Above, with Mexican President Ernesto Zedillo in Mexico City. The return of refugees to Guatemala and the Chiapas crisis are frequent topics between both presidents. Left, with Honduran President Carlos Roberto Reina. Below, signing a bilateral agreement with U.S. Ambassador Marilyn McAfee.

With United Nations Secretary General Boutros Boutros-Ghali during his visit to Guatemala.

With Costa Rican President José María Figueres. President De León Carpio has maintained cordial relations with the region's presidents.

With Education Minister Celestino Tay Coyoy, first indigenous minister in Guatemala's history, and Finance Minister Ana de Molina, the architect of tax reform.

With Ricardo San Pedro at the Aurora Air Force Base, while waiting for the remains of his cousin Jorge Carpio.

After the crisis generated by former President Serrano's self-coup was resolved, the nation's principal leaders spoke to the press at the main hall of the Government Palace in Guatemala. From left, Ramiro de León Carpio, then-Human Rights Commissioner; an unidentified person; Jorge Mario García La Guardia, of the Constitutional Court (currently Human Rights Commissioner); Gen. Jorge Perussina, then-Defense Chief of Staff; Epaminondas González, who was president of the Constitutional Court; Gen. José Domingo García Samayoa, then-Defense Minister; Carlos Reinoso Gil, of the Constitutional Court (currently Interior Minister); and Gen. Mario Enríquez, Deputy Defense Chief of Staff (currently Defense Minister).

Generals José Domingo García (extreme left), José Luis Quilo (center), and Jorge Perussina (left), were dismissed from the Guatemalan Army by President Ramiro de León Carpio.

Guerrilla commanders Rolando Morán, Pablo Monsanto and Rodrigo Asturias, alias Gaspar Ilom, talk to the press.

Arriving at the National Palace to demand that constitutional order be restored. President Serrano was president.

Enjoying an outdoor community event with Vice-president Arturo Herbruger Asturias.

With (from left) Mrs. Tere de Zarco, co-owner of Guatemala's most important newspaper, Prensa Libre; *First Lady María Eugenia de De León; and the paper's editor José Eduardo Zarco.*

The presidency has not kept Ramiro de León Carpio, an enthusiastic soccer fan, from practicing his favorite sport.

Right, at a work session with Chief of Staff Gen. Otto Pérez Molina. Below, taking the presidential oath.

The President talks with Pope John Paul II during a visit to the Vatican in Rome.

Photo by Nuri Vallbona/The Miami Herald

Above, at the Vizcaya Palace on Dec. 10, 1994, during the Summit of the Americas held in Miami, Florida. To his left, Presidents Bill Clinton (USA), Carlos Roberto Reina (Honduras), Violeta Chamorro (Nicaragua), and Prime Minister Manuel Esquivel (Belize). Right, in his presidential office at the National Palace.

A Failed Coup

President Jorge Serrano attempted a coup d'etat from the presidency on May 25, 1993 to usurp congressional and judicial powers and take full control of the nation from his executive office. People took to the streets and political leaders came out in defense of the Constitution. President Serrano (left) called a press conference to announce his move. People on the streets (below) protested.

Guatemalan newspapers' coverage of President Serrano's self-coup attempt had prominent front-page placement and carried large headlines clamoring for the President's resignation. In the photo, street demonstrators displayed newspaper pages as banners in their vigorous protest.

The Guatemalan Congress aborted the crisis by declaring President Serrano's action unconstitutional and dismissing him from office. It then elected Ramiro de León Carpio to lead the nation for the remainder of the term. In the photo, the new President salutes the crowd after taking oath.

9

Cleaning Up the House

Question: *Let's go back to a fascinating topic. You were elected President by a Congress in which there were members whom you yourself considered corrupt. How aware were you of this situation?*

Ramiro de León Carpio: That was a serious problem to which it was hard to find a solution. Right after assuming the presidency I took a trip through the countryside. I went back to many places I had visited as Human Rights Commissioner. Visiting them again as President and Commander in Chief forced me to be totally sincere. I informed people of my government program, elaborating on my intentions to achieve institutional stability and eliminate the ghost of the recurring *coup d'etat*.

I had secretly set myself a 180-day deadline to settle into power, but long before that period expired the popular clamor for cleaning up the legislative branch began. I had to do something. In a speech I made during one of my trips in the municipality of Melchor de Mencos in the Petén Province I announced a purge through legitimate means and publicly asked the Congressmen to purge themselves.

Q: *Was there much pressure to close Congress?*

RDLC: Yes, both from the people and the media. Far from opposing it, the military supported such measure. Everywhere I went, people would say: "Fire them, Mr. President, fire them. We'll go with you to oust them." That was the popular clamor. So, my speech was a joyful piece against corruption, but I told them I would act through legal means.

This I reiterated later in a historical speech broadcast nationwide on radio and television, in which I asked Congressmen to resign so that the purging process could commence. I officially embarked in a campaign to cleanse government from its corrupt elements. The media and the people backed me. Support came from various sources and the military did not interfere nor pressured me.

But there were problems. The more honest segment of Congress failed in an attempt to get rid of the corrupt through a coup of sorts. Seeing that they would not resign I resorted to the legal mechanism of proposing a referendum to the Electoral Supreme Court, a measure established by the Constitution.

The idea was to consult with the people whether they wanted the Congressmen to stay or not, whether they preferred to move up legislative elections. The Electoral Supreme Court gave me the green light to consult the people, but when I set a date for the referendum, the Constitutional Court, clinging to a series of technicalities, blocked it. This awakened again the rumors of a coup.

Q: *Was there a strong threat from the military?*

RDLC: Not really. Only rumors, civilians knocking on barrack doors, etc. Rumors. Nothing concrete, even at the most difficult moment.

You have to remember the conditions in which I received the country. I had inherited a totally bankrupt country, plagued with debts and in financial chaos. Yet accomplishing an investment percentage of 68, which later we raised to 76 percent of the budget.

I was fighting battles on many fronts. Acting in complete transparence, I immersed simultaneously in the fight against poverty and in an all-out effort to strengthen the institutions. Finally, the situation became serious and I accepted the mediation of the Catholic Church, which obtained Congress' consent for amending the Constitution to interrupt the mandate of legislators. I have to imagine that Congressmen didn't realize what they were signing, for it meant their way out of office.

The agreement led us to constitutional amendments which ended the legislative term, and a popular referendum was called to comply with the Constitution's requisite of consulting the people on certain issues. On its dogmatic part — human rights clauses, for instance — the Guatemalan Constitution can only be amended by the Constitutional Assembly. The rest of it, with the exception of certain unamendable articles, can be amended by a vote of two thirds of Congress backed by a popular referendum.

The amendments addressed, among other issues, the constitutional mandate of Congress and the Supreme Court, calling for new elections to both bodies. They eliminated the President's so-called confidential funds, a measure the entire nation applauded. The privileges of Congressmen also disappeared. Before these reforms, for example, Congressmen accused of any crime would receive a preliminary trial in which they themselves acted as both defendant and judge. No longer. All these measures tended to end political impunity, especially among Congressmen.

A new procedure was designed to elect the General Accountant, the person who oversees public spending, to grant him complete independence and autonomy. Similar procedures were established to give absolute independence to the Attorney General and the General Prosecutor, separating these two bodies and turning the latter into a government counsel while redefining the tasks of the Attorney General more in the area of prosecuting in behalf of society.

Official currency could no longer be issued without the Central Bank's support, except in special cases authorized by Congress. This eliminated the perpetual danger of inflation caused by the abuse of prior governments.

All these initiatives I as President submitted to Congress. All tended to do away with political impunity and corruption. They were all positive measures accepted within the framework of the political agreement signed through the Catholic Church's mediation and later approved by Congress after much international pressure and popular clamor.

Q: *Didn't the media criticize you for reaching an agreement with the Congressmen instead of dissolving Congress and taking them to court?*

RDLC: Yes, but I would never have taken any action violating the Constitution and the democratic system. A segment of the media was very upset and demanded that Congress be closed. I opted to call for the referendum to ratify the constitutional amendments and went on a national tour to mobilize the people into participating. Politicians had traditionally been so discredited that people had little enthusiasm.

It made me so sad. In other parts of the world there's always interest in any election, particularly local and for mayor. Not here. Even if this vote came down to a yes-or-no decision, people didn't understand the issues. There had been little time to explain what was going on, and certain individuals used this circumstance to deliberately misinform and confuse. It thus became necessary for the President, with all his credibility and the backing behind him, to travel through the countryside explaining what it was all about.

The defining moment came on Sunday January 30, 1994, and, because of the reasons mentioned, the turnout was dismal. Only 17 percent of the voters showed up at the polls, 93 percent of which approved the amendments.

Q: *Such a poor turnout must have weakened you. Did it have a political impact?*

RDLC: At that moment, yes. There was criticism from conflicting groups and from the press, which aired irresponsible disappointment and stirred things in an effort to turn the positive into a negative.

I believe the voters didn't show for other reasons as well — lack of transportation, for instance. In general elections the political parties provide transportation. On this occasion the political parties did absolutely nothing. After all, this was only an open vote, honest, pure, legitimate, not convenient for them at all.

In certain ways, you can say it was a negative vote. Yet in politics only the actual results really matter. Today nobody remembers the turnout percentage. The fact remains that on January 30, 1994, people said yes to a popular referendum to amend the Constitution, kicking corrupt Congressmen and magistrates out of office.

Some Congressmen tried to cling to their office using the low turnout as an argument to invalidate the amendments. They alleged it was not legitimate to amend the Constitution based on a minority vote. In other words, after the referendum came the most difficult part — the confrontation with Congress. They tried to stay in office through all kinds of legal and illegal moves. Some appealed to the Constitutional Court and other tribunals, though in the end the vote became irreversible. The popular clamor left no room for backing out in spite of the legal and illegal mechanisms utilized. Time kept running short and, finally, when the deadline of August 15 came, the constitutional amendments became final.

Q: *That was the date on which the new Congress was to be elected. Was it not?*

RDLC: No. That was the date in which the House was to be dissolved. Elections for a new Congress took place on September 14. After the new Congress took office, the new Supreme Court was installed. The purge was thus accomplished without shedding one drop of blood. At that moment, all criticism turned into praise. That's life. I guess it was finally understood that I had taken a longer and more difficult road, an alternative that turned out to be the correct, legal and democratic way. Although I feel this as a personal triumph, it was a victory for the people of Guatemala. The period of political cleansing had ended and present and future stability had been achieved. This had been my second goal after accomplishing my first goal of rescuing and strengthening the institutional and democratic system.

10

War and Peace

Question: *You attained a new Congress, but on the table remained one of the nation's old problems. I'm referring to the guerrillas. How did peace talks with the guerrillas begin?*
Ramiro de León Carpio: The talks began under Vinicio Cerezo's presidency and they have been prolonged intermittently. At this time we have reached some preliminary agreements and I don't know where negotiations will lead. Sometimes people ask me why we are talking with the guerrillas now that the Cold War is over, when the guerrilla's ideological, psychological and even economic ammunition have ceased to exist or have been considerably diminished; when subversion is no longer a serious problem nor there exists a question of military equality to justify such talks. Why negotiate with guerrillas? Why give them more institutional importance than they actually have?

I would have to begin by saying that when I took office the first issue the international community presented to me was to resolve the guerrilla problem. Not the Guatemalans, though. To them the guerrillas were no longer an important problem.

As a President who was once the Human Rights Commissioner, I didn't rank the guerrillas as my first priority. Our first goal was to avoid more *coups d'etat* and rescue an institutionality that had been shattered. The international media did not understand this and criticized me. After a delay of two, three months, I put together a National Peace Plan.

Negotiations had begun three years before I became President. When I took office I found that these talks had stalled and were not making progress. The Catholic Church, especially its conciliator, Msgr. Rodolfo Quezada Toruño, had made extraordinary efforts and the conversations had begun, but the box of agreements was completely empty.

The guerrillas are not a confrontational threat. It's not like they will reach power or occupy territory. No. It's a force with great limitations. One day they blow up an electrical tower somewhere and cause a blackout for a few hours; another day they destroy a bridge we later rebuild with some help from the private sector. They destroy; we build. Yet another day there may be an encounter in which one of our patrols is attacked, killing or wounding soldiers or officers. All sporadic, since they have no permanent presence. Of course these are human lives, but they do not represent a risk for the nation.

The guerrilla issue has two negative effects for which we must end the confrontation. One, it's the primary source of human rights violations. Once this conflict ends, human rights violations will diminish considerably. There will be, of course, as in any other place in the world, isolated cases of police brutality. But that's what the courts are for; that's what the Human Rights Commissioner is all about.

The other effect of the guerrilla movement is that it diverts our time and concentration from addressing other grave problems, such as social and economic development. Like other underdeveloped countries, Guatemala faces many problems. Were it not for the guerrillas, Guatemala, with all its favorable elements, could take off easily into its journey to resolve its social needs.

This is why I submitted a National Peace Plan and made a commitment to implement it. I could have said: "Well, guys, the process is over. If you want to incorporate into the system, throw away your weapons and be done with it." But that would have caused me international trouble, even if the reality is that militarily the guerrillas are defeated.

Q: *In what way are they militarily defeated?*

RDLC: There are no more than 1,000 guerrillas in the entire country. Besides, a guerrilla war must have a base, popular support. Day by day, with every action they keep losing every possibility of support. Moreover, we are fighting poverty, taking our work to the countryside, especially in areas of armed conflict. This reduces the number of people willing to support them. People resent the fighting more and more every day; they demand peace.

Q: *Historically, guerrillas have been strong in the Department of Quiché, where there is a large indigenous presence and an acute concentration of poverty. Are you saying they no longer enjoy the support of El Quiché?*

RDLC: Yes, that's what I'm referring to. I have just inaugurated the Peace Highway from Atitlán Lake to the village of Chichicastenango, two high tourist areas. That highway runs through places where there was once intense fighting. Today you can ride through it without a worry. There are no more guerrillas in the area. In fact, I believe El Quiché is the place where guerrillas are hated the most because it's where more blood was shed.

When I took office people were asking me for peace. "Mr. President, we want to be allowed to work in peace and freedom." It's what they wanted. They were nauseated by war and violence, and they knew they could improve their life and their children's life through their work, the marketing of their produce. It's an irreversible fact that armed conflict has no place in Guatemala.

Why then do I keep negotiating with them? Because I believe it's indispensable to avoid extermination. I don't want those thousand men still fighting exterminated, because it would be a loss of human lives, many human rights violations, and more blood uselessly shed by Guatemalans. This is why I submitted to the people of Guatemala and later to the international community a National Peace Plan comprising three main points: First, national reconciliation. In so many years of war deep wounds have been opened and the Guatemalan family has been divided. We must, for example, assist in the return of refugees, who come back to a hostile environment far from peaceful. It's not easy. There are ideological and sociological problems. Reconciliation is not easy, really. There is also the problem of uprooted people who had to flee their place of origin overwhelmed by violence and now wish to come home.

Secondly, my plan includes fighting poverty. There's the important battle worth fighting. We should care about this aspect. In vain will we sign a peace treaty if poverty is not fought and injustice persists. New socially discontent groups could emerge in the future, as has happened to Mexico in Chiapas with the Zapatista National Liberation Army. Peace is not only the absence of war. Economic and social peace are also needed. By tackling poverty and implementing economic, social and cultural rights, we guarantee that the peace we sign is durable.

And the third point is precisely the end of the internal armed conflict. With this plan I salute and thank Msgr. Quezada Toruño for his participation. He had played a significant role and his efforts had reached a limit. My idea then incorporated the international community through United Nations and the group of friendly nations we created with Venezuela, Colombia, Mexico, the United States, Spain and Norway.

Q: *Did you believe Msgr. Quezada Toruño's negotiation could go no further?*

RDLC: It was totally stagnated, though not because of his inability or that of the Church. On the contrary, Msgr. Quezada Toruño played a fundamental role in this process, but it had reached a dead end. Pressure was needed on both sides, the government and the guerrillas, and it needed the weight of an organization like the United Nations. And this is what has gotten us closer to peace — the participation of the United Nations and the group of nations friendly to the peace process. It led to significant progress during the first six months of 1994 after we signed the Marco Agreement in January committing ourselves to sign a peace treaty. The psychological impact of this prompted eight guerrilla fighters to turn themselves in and weakened the subversive movement.

This progress led to other accords, such as a basic global pact on human rights; and agreements on relocating uprooted populations, on timetable, on the creation of the Historical Clarification Commission, on Immediate International Verification which created MINUGUA, the United Nations mission operating in the country with more than 400 people verifying on site the compliance with human rights by both sides — guerrillas and government forces. And, last though probably the most important and complex of all, the Accord on Identity and Rights of Indigenous Populations.

Q: *Did the Truth Commission, charged with establishing what really happened all these years, come from these accords?*

RDLC: Yes, the Truth Commission's real name is the Historical Clarification Commission. There's also an accord to verify the cease-fire, which is the one that brought the United Nations to Guatemala. This marked a significant development in the situation, for the United Nations's presence facilitates verification of anything.

Q: *Do you consider a failure the fact that a peace treaty has not yet been signed with the guerrillas?*

RDLC: Undoubtedly. For Guatemalans it's a failure from the humanitarian standpoint, among other reasons. There's still violence out there. Every life saved is important. We don't want more widows, more orphans, more tears. We're talking about human life here. I personally would have liked not to have lost one second, and I went all out to speed up the process. Unfortunately, there have been delays and, yes, it can be considered a failure. Lives could have been saved and we would have had more time to deal with poverty and other issues. I could have taken another attitude. I could have said, "Well, we couldn't do this and the guerrillas are to blame. End of the process." But I don't want to carry that historical responsibility. I will not get up from the negotiating table until we have signed a peace treaty. It's my strategy, my political decision to persevere until the end.

Q: *You appointed Héctor Rosada as chairman of the Peace Commission. Could you tell us who he is, and why you named him and gave him that responsibility?*

RDLC: When I decided to present a new National Peace Plan I had to find a person capable of moving the peace negotiations forward. The peace process is hard to explain. There has been a lot of progress, but if a peace treaty is not signed, the cease-fire will be useless. I have much clarity on this. The guerrillas have their own strategy and they are finding it difficult to incorporate into national life. The commanders are not known, and do not enjoy popular support. In El Salvador, for example, the guerrillas had some popular support, and they had 30,000 to 40,000 armed men. Here we're talking about 1,000 people trying to put together a political party for which they will need support. There lies a logistical undercurrent that somehow pushes them to continue the war.

Amid the difficulties inherent to the process I believed the best person to lead this effort was Héctor Rosada. A man who has been labeled as a leftist, but who is a highly versatile individual — a sociologist, historian, anthropologist, attorney, and above all a researcher. This is a person who has devoted his life to research, to find the truth wherever it may be. No other person knows the Guatemalan reality as thoroughly as he does — psychologically, anthropologically and historically.

Q: *It's been said that he was very close to the guerrillas. Do you see that as an advantage?*

RDLC: Of course. He was close to them because of his scientific and academic research, which is fundamentally why I chose him. When he faces the guerrillas, he knows them perfectly well, he knows their rhetoric, their tactics, their behavior, their train of thought. At the same time, he is an absolutely mature person. I appointed him without consulting with the military, which proves I am not in the hands of the military. I named him because I considered him to be the right choice, period. I can imagine there may have been some resentment and concerns among people in the armed forces because they knew him; he had lectured the military on academic topics.

I knew Rosada from his writings and lectures. I had met him personally in the university and I trusted his great qualifications. He was a skilled negotiator who handled terminology well and was knowledgeable on the topics to be discussed. Although he had been somewhat close to the guerrillas, he wasn't a Marxist and didn't share their ideas nor their illegal armed approach to political change. And he was familiar with the thinking process of 50 years ago, which to me is the fundamental problem of the guerrillas — that they are still infatuated with a discourse that dates half-a-century back.

The Beauty and the Killer

By Santiago Aroca

How does a frail, well-educated American woman fall for a Mayan guerrilla fighter notorious among his adversaries for his tough, ruthless, merciless ways?

It was an unusual story. They met in a rebel camp on the side of a volcano — he slightly agitated with a machete hanging from his shoulder though smiling and reluctant to leave; she in awe at the sight of a real guerrilla commander.

Jennifer Harbury, a Harvard lawyer, was 39 when she met Efraín Bámaca, a 35-year-old Indian turned warrior under the name of *Comandante Everardo*. She was writing a book on the role of women in the Guatemalan guerrillas and had traveled from Texas to Mexico. She later crossed to Guatemala, to the jungles in the west of the country.

Her project had no pretension of objectivity. She knew that the guerrillas were killing soldiers, Indians and everyone who stood in the way. She knew there was a war going on in Guatemala.

Bámaca had a reputation for being a ferocious combatant, though famed among his adversaries as a ruthless, sanguinary killer. He was the only Mayan Indian to become a guerrilla commander. Born in a humble farm, he learned to read at the age of 18 after joining the guerrillas. The war was his only school.

To the Guatemalan government Bámaca is nothing but a terrorist, a man on the run for 17 years for murder and theft. And Harbury was but an adventurer they liked to describe as a bored, rich woman trying to put together her life after a failed marriage.

Of course, there are many versions to this story, depending on who is telling it. Harbury rejects the Guatemalan government's accusations and insists she has no regrets. When she just saw Bámaca she was surprised at his youth. She expected someone older, rather ugly and unappealing. He wasn't so to her.

In interviews given in Washington and in Guatemala, Harbury described Bámaca as an attractive man, full of charm and humanity. She even referred to him as frail and as delicate as a snowflake. Of course he knew death was always at his heels, just as she realized her own life was marked by boredom.

According to Harbury, they both felt mutual attraction, although nothing happened on that occasion. It was not until after a year, when they saw each other again in Mexico, that love clicked. They married in 1991 in a Texas home, a union that attorneys hired by the Guatemalan government argue was never legally registered. She will not hear about such details, finding ground in the guerrilla tradition of exchanging spoons rather than rings.

Bámaca disappeared in an ambush by Guatemalan armed forces on March 12, 1992. It took Harbury more than three years to learn, from U.S. congressional sources, what exactly had happened to her husband.

In April of 1995, Rep. Robert Torricelli, Democrat for New Jersey, sent a letter to President Bill Clinton accusing the CIA of operating out of control. Torricelli said that, according to documentary evidence he had gathered, a colonel of the Guatemalan army, paid by the CIA, had supervised the torture sessions on Bámaca and had ordered the guerrilla commander's murder. Torricelli's statement shook the Washington's establishment and unleashed a chain of investigations.

Curiously, Torricelli had a bad name among the Latin American left for having authored a bill passed in 1992 to dramatically toughen the embargo the United States had imposed on the Cuban government in the early 60s. To some observers, Torricelli's interest in this issue derived from his desire to be perceived as a true liberal within the U.S. political spectrum.

In any case, to Harbury, Torricelli's statement ended three years of pain, uncertainty and fear. She reiterated she would pursue her search of Bámaca's remains to give them an appropriate burial.

In Guatemala she was hardly understood. "Who could believe that a woman who ate caviar and frequented high-society parties in Boston would fall for a guerrilla fighter who killed soldiers, civilians and cattle, and who stole from his own compatriots?" wrote a well known columnist in Guatemala, implying that Harbury's motivation had to be money.

Yet money never appeared, and Harbury insists that theirs was a true love story. And although all love stories are different and exceptional, Harbury's has been enveloped by a special sadness.

Even before disappearing in the jungle, he had warned her that their time together would be short, she says. That's why they never said good-bye, fearing that it would be like an omen.

When the couple met in 1990 Harbury already was well informed about Guatemala from the time she had helped human rights organizations in the United States. That work gained her the trust of the guerrillas, who rarely admitted foreigners in their military camps.

She was eventually allowed to visit rebel territory. She had agreed with the guerrillas to meet in a village where she was received by barefooted and poorly dressed Indians. Outside the village, the Indians changed into uniforms and they walked with her through the mountains for eight hours. In her interviews she got to know the guerrilla commander well. She watched him give orders and train the younger soldiers. Night after night, while the rest of the men slept under the stars, Harbury asked him about his life, about his loves and his commitment. Bámaca answered some of her questions and asked a few questions himself. He asked her about her family, about her father, the chemistry professor in Dartmouth, about her sister Katerina, an anthropologist born deaf who went to school with her.

Harbury spoke nonstop about her younger brothers — Olin, the doctor, and Alex, the computer expert. She told him about her education at Cornell, where she learned a little Chinese, and at Harvard, where she received a law degree.

He in turn told her of the years

when as a child he worked the corn fields; and how at age 18 he had known the son of Nobel laureate Miguel Angel Asturias, Rodrigo Asturias, known as *Comandante Gaspar Ilom,* who led a guerrilla group; and how he ended up joining another group, the Organization of the People in Arms (ORPA). He told her the revolution had taught him everything he knew because he had never gone to school.

According to Harbury, he worried that she would not be faithful. She only feared that he would get killed. They married on September 25, 1991, before eight friends. No priest ministered in the ceremony, nor was there a judge present, but in their hearts it was a true wedding. Harbury translated into English.

One of her friends, Emily Jones, said she had never seen Harbury so happy. Immediately after the wedding, the couple traveled to Mexico, where they rented an apartment. They spent their time in bed, reading and not talking much. They would go out into the city, and they would even go dancing, though he didn't like that very much. She cooked, which was something she hated. One afternoon he took a piece of paper and drew a plan of how to build a refuge to hide from bombings. To Harbury this was love, a profound love that never led to quarrels.

There was a war in Guatemala and Bámaca heard about the death of some of his buddies, comrades in arms in so many battles. He also read stories that ran in Guatemalan newspapers profiling him as a common criminal. One day he said he had to go. Harbury understood and did not oppose him. She only said that they would see each other in a few months, but he didn't answer.

Harbury was the first to leave Mexico. She traveled to New Hampshire where her best friend was dying of cancer. Shortly afterward, he packed. He took all the photos and love letters and buried them in a sealed can at the border. He later wrote her a letter and then there was a long silence.

One day someone called from Mexico to tell her there was a problem, that he needed to see her urgently. Harbury packed in a hurry and went to Mexico, where she was informed that Bámaca's unit had been ambushed by a military patrol. The shock made her lose the baby she was carrying.

Nothing happened for over a year until in 1992 a guerrilla escaped from a military detention center and fled to Mexico. He said he had seen Bámaca alive and had watched how they tortured him. She believed him and challenged the official version that assured Bámaca had died in combat. The military took her to a tomb where they said Bámaca was buried. But she wouldn't know the real story of what happened until April of 1995 in Washington. When she heard it she broke down in tears.

Shortly after, two U.S. senators addressed the President asking him to provide special FBI protection to Harbury. They alleged that the Guatemalan military had a plan to assassinate her. U.S. State Department spokeswoman Julie Reside confirmed she had information about possible assassination attempts against Harbury. "We have alerted the Guatemalan government that, if anything happened, it would be grave," she said.

Guatemalan President Ramiro de León Carpio told the press that his government had taken all appropriate measures to protect Jennifer Harbury and to punish those who made any attempt against her. Further, President De León Carpio instructed the nation's general prosecutor to open an investigation and to punish all members of the military who may be found guilty.

So far, Harbury has suffered no harm and she is busy writing the screenplay for a film about her love story with the Guatemalan guerrilla. It's difficult to believe, though, that there would be any reference in her story about the suffering and pain of the families that lost their loved ones in combat, or even of the peaceful, hard-working Indians trapped in the crossfire of two adversary camps that submerged the nation in a valley of death and desolation. Love has such mysterious ways.

11

The Guerrillas' Outdated Discourse

Question: *You say the guerrillas' discourse is outdated; yet you concede that misery prevails, precisely the poverty which prompted many to rise in arms in the mountains.*

Ramiro de León Carpio: Yes, but the situation is very different. Let me give you an example of something that happened recently in Guatemala. A well-known farm was paying its workers a wage below the minimum established by law in this country. The owners tried to justify the policy arguing workers received part of their compensation in goods. A big public debate resulted and the Defense Minister intervened in favor of the workers calling on the owners to correct the situation immediately. Imagine! The Defense Minister confronting the business sector.

The minister was totally right. He made the point that either the law was complied with or we would end up facing a violent outburst prompted by the existing misery. Peasants are not to be exploited. In the context of the discourse of 50 years ago, such line of reasoning would have conformed exclusively to subversion. Not today. Today we speak the same language. Businessmen, workers, the military, the President — all coincide in that such behavior must not be permitted any longer.

I'm not overly concerned about the termination of the domestic armed conflict because, be it now or later, it is bound to end. It would be regrettable if it didn't end soon, what with all the human lives affected. Yet peace is irreversible, nothing can stop it now. I am concerned, however, about the advent of peace. As things stand now, people have learned to raise their voice in freedom to claim their rights. For this we must prepare ourselves; it's where the real risk lies. Not only morally, but spiritually and economically as well. The moment peace arrives in Guatemala, only tourism will be ready to take off, and we need to be ready lest the outburst of peace overwhelms us. The social consequence may very well lead to a surge of violence.

Q: *What is your opinion of the guerrilla commanders? Is there one whom you feel personal respect for?*

RDLC: To me the one with the most outstanding personality is Miguel Angel Asturias's son, Rodrigo Asturias, whose war name is *Comandante Gaspar Ilom.*

Q: *Do you believe his father, the great Guatemalan writer Miguel Angel Asturias, would have made a guerrilla leader?*

RDLC: I don't think so. Asturias's ideas reflected reality. He had the ability to depict crudely though gently the reality of our dictatorships. He was also a great journalist. In fact, I was told he started out as a journalist devoted to radio broadcasting. He later entered the field of literature and told the story of Guatemala. Told us, for example, what the figure of the president represented in the era of Manuel Estrada Cabrera's dictatorship.

No, I don't believe Asturias would have risen up in arms. He was often viewed as a communist, though in his time people saw communists even in their soups.

The main problem guerrilla leaders have had is their inability to reach power after more than 30 years of struggle or to adapt to social changes. They believed the indigenous community would support them and that hasn't happened. I know Guatemalan Indians well and I have been close to their reality.

Q: *What is the difference between the indigenous community you know and the one the guerrillas depict?*

RDLC: First, the indigenous population they knew was a closed, non-participating community, totally hermetic. The culture of participation Indians have today is unprecedented. They are communicative and knowledgeable. Moreover, they are sociologically and historically represented by genuine indigenous professionals who have educated themselves. Authentic leaders, not the vociferous individuals who come out on television. Today, indigenous leaders are better known than any of the guerrilla commanders.

On the other hand, today's indigenous community is nonconformist. The one they knew never dared to protest. Not so today. Now they are not so agreeable, they want to get ahead, they see the opportunity of economic development before them and they want to take it. In my administration, for instance, national education has been in the hands of two Indians — the Education Minister, Dr. Celestino Alfredo Tay Coyoy, and the Vice-Minister, Manuel de Jesús Salazar Tezahuic. They are both scientists, educators, sociologists, historians, who know the indigenous reality better than anybody else. They are in charge of education at a national level, something unthinkable a few years back.

I remember that when I took office I was asked to create an indigenous office and a ministry. What was necessary, however, was that one, two, four Indians became cabinet members. I chose the Ministry of Education because of bilingual education. Our problem is that 60 percent of the population is Indian and needed to be educated in Spanish and in their own language. This never entered the minds of guerrilla commanders. They called this a counterinsurgent ploy. They thought the same of the Indigenous Development Fund. Another project even more foreign to guerrillas is the forest program, organized by the most active entities in the indigenous community to protect the environment.

In 40 years things have changed and the guerrillas have remained frozen in time, locked in their 40-year-old discourse and in a reality unknown to them. That's their main problem. They need to incorporate into that reality, which would constitute a positive move for Guatemala.

Q: *How representative of the indigenous community is Nobel Peace laureate Rigoberta Menchú?*

RDLC: I feel a lot of appreciation for Rigoberta. I met her, traveled with her. I have a lot of admiration for her efforts, for what she has done. From the standpoint of knowledge, she is not very representative. She has the following of human rights activists and leaders, but she is not one who draws big crowds. Other leaders, yes; not she. Unfortunately, she has not been capable of capitalizing on her Nobel Peace Prize.

Rigoberta could have been a key player in the Guatemalan reconciliation and in the process of national reunification. But she has adopted a negative attitude and a discourse unfavorable to Guatemala. As I see it, she had the support of the guerrillas in the circumstance she faced when leaving Nicaragua and, obviously, she is grateful to those who helped her. She has acknowledged that the guerrillas and their European supporters came to her help. But when she received the Nobel Prize, she should have distanced from them. It's like when a President must speak for the entire nation.

I say this with much respect. It would have been good if she had taken a position above all good and evil and devoted her time to reconciliation. Yet she withdrew, even at the moment of Serrano's self-coup. Rigoberta was one of a few leaders who withdrew only to reappear later with a destructive discourse. A crass political mistake. All segments of society united to resolve the problem, and she is viewed in Guatemala as someone who did not make a contribution, did not give the Nobel Prize its true value and significance. I regret it because she could have been a fundamental element in our peace process.

Q: *Have you read her books?*
RDLC: Oh, yes. I have some of them personally autographed.
Q: *Do you like them?*
RDLC: Of course. They are a poetic narrative that touches you, both exciting and depressing. I like her writing, her style. Her efforts are indeed most admirable. The times I've had to knock on doors asking for international help haven't been easy. I did it before becoming President, when I was with the Atanasio Tzul Institute. It's difficult to get doors opened at high levels in Europe and in the United States. I have gone through that experience, and I admire her. The doors she is capable of opening and the circles in which she moves show an extraordinary effort. I have read her work with great objectivity.
Q: *Rigoberta Menchú directs much criticism to your policy of relocating displaced families. She argues it is contrary to Indian interests. How do you feel about this?*
RDLC: Relocation is one of the fundamental points of the peace program. When we talk about relocation we are talking reconciliation, and that's the most difficult aspect of this issue. I experienced the division of the Guatemalan family for 34 years. Some of us were on this side of the border; the others were in Mexico. Those who were displaced — approximately one million people — now want to relocate.

I was the first to travel with some diplomats to visit the Communities of People in Resistance (CPR). These are people who left 10 years ago to distance themselves from the climate of violence and ended up in inhospitable places where they suffered severe hardship. I was commissioner then and our visit had to be coordinated with the guerrillas. My first message was that they could return but that they would have to acknowledge the authorities. For years they heard the worst things about the armed forces, and it was hard for them to accept the military. They finally did. They had a truly harsh life. Some couldn't even go down to the villages and had to eat only what they themselves were able to grow. They lived a very primitive, underdeveloped life. With time, we eventually got them to also repudiate the guerrillas.

In my conversations with them I used analogies to illustrate my points. I would tell them: "What happens when two of you get drunk and begin fighting each other? Whom are you both harming? The people surrounding you would be in danger. A child, a woman. So what do you do? You separate them from the rest so they can go elsewhere to fight, or stop fighting altogether. The same happens with the guerrillas and the army. You insist the army must be distanced. Why don't you ask that both, the guerrillas and the army, be distanced? If you ask that only the army leave, it would be logical to think that you want the guerrillas to stay. They both fight, they both shoot their weapons, they both do harm to those surrounding them." With this simple message I began working with those communities and today they accept the concept. They moved significantly forward when they said they didn't want more confrontation. These are hard-working people who live in highly productive land, constantly harassed with no laws to protect them. Their children have grown without schooling. Slowly, they began to return, first to again cultivate their land which is what they do best. Now they just want to return to the place where they were born and their parents are buried.

Q: *How many people are awaiting relocation?*

RDLC: About a million people were displaced, but many have already returned. Some have been relocated. There's a political angle to this as well as economic. The economic aspect is to bring them home to their land. If they return to a place occupied by others who took over the land when they left, there are two alternatives. Find a place for those who are occupying the land and reach an agreement, which is not easy; or find a new place for those returning, which is also difficult, since they feel they have a right to their land, as do the others.

This is the key to reconciliation. A situation similar is that of the refugees, which is another topic. Of the 45,000 refugees, approximately 20,000 have returned and have received property titles. Now not only do they have the land but also the property title, meaning they can do anything they want with it.

It will be difficult for these people to support the guerrillas. They have their land and do not want trouble. All they want upon their return is to work the land and live in peace, without the suffering and problems they had for so long.

Q: *What would happen if the peace agreement is signed?*

RDLC: If the peace agreement is signed they will have jobs, roads, financial aid, credit, technology, marketing assistance. These are hard-working, business-oriented people who have asked me and bankers about exporting non-traditional products. They don't need much to get ahead, but they want peace. If the peace treaty is signed the political problem would be out of the way. If not, both the refugees and the relocated people will have problems.

Q: *In other words, if the peace agreement is not signed the relocation program would be frozen.*

RDLC: Somehow, yes. Those who volunteer would continue to relocate, but a massive relocation could not be permitted due to the danger of guerrilla infiltration. There has to be a cease-fire, and guerrillas would have to be demobilized and disarmed.

That's why it's important to sign the peace agreement. If this cannot be achieved, things would get bad. You see, there is feud and resentment. The returning refugee thinks the government gives more help to the one who stayed behind. And the one who remained in place begins to realize that the returning refugee is getting international help. The bottom line is that both will protest.

The only solution is to fight poverty. That's what I call carrying out the revolution — a moral revolution, peaceful, without weapons — to turn Guatemala around and make it a just society. The only revolution I believe in is the battle against corruption and poverty through participation. Otherwise, this country will not change, no matter how much international aid it receives, regardless of all the help government is willing to give.

That's my primary message — to tell people that to change our country their opinion is important and their participation indispensable. This message has gradually permeated society to the point that, when I visit a village and people ask for running water and I am told it costs 400,000 quetzals (approximately $100,000), the community contributes 100,000. A really poor community commits itself to contribute 100,000 quetzals in three or four months. Then I try to get the municipalities to contribute 100,000, and maybe Japan's embassy another 100,000, and then the government grants the remainder. This type of participation turns the community into a watchdog, controlling and making sure not one penny is stolen. That is what could reform Guatemala.

Another important principle is decentralization. We have made some progress decentralizing administrative functions and supporting local authorities so that decisions would come up from the base instead of going down from the upper echelons of government. At the base, for example, teachers should be appointed by parents under the supervision of mayors. That system is already in place. What could be more effective than parents supervising teachers and making sure they do their jobs well?

We're also decentralizing health care, empowering community organizations to manage their hospitals. We have also decentralized the economy, transferring resources to the countryside and to the poorest and neediest in the most remote of places. And, finally, fiscal decentralization is also functioning, with taxes collected locally and its proceeds reverted to the community that generated them.

Q: *While Guatemala improves its economic development, what is Mexico's role in the guerrillas? To put it bluntly, does Mexico support Guatemalan guerrillas?*

RDLC: Mexico has a very peculiar policy toward all Latin American countries and the United States. In the case of Guatemala, they have given sanctuary to the guerrillas. Because of Mexico's foreign policy, guerrillas have been greeted in Mexican territory, from where they have returned through the border to launch attacks against us. Our common border makes it possible for guerrillas to seek temporary refuge on the other side to later return to Guatemalan territory. Curious that with the Zapatistas Mexico is suffering what we suffered before. But none of this has kept our countries from enjoying excellent relations, both commercially and politically. Especially in recent years, since the beginning of the Guatemalan democratic experiment.

Common borders generate problems in all countries. There have been historic wars over territorial claims. The United States seized part of California from Mexico. Mexico in turn seized Chiapas from us. This type of problem has come to be logical and normal.

Q: *If Mexico denied sanctuary to guerrillas, would this problem end?*

RDLC: Sure. We have this agreement in Central America that no country can grant refuge to people planning to attack a neighboring nation. So guerrillas couldn't find refuge in Central American countries, such as El Salvador, Nicaragua, Costa Rica, etc. Ironic that Mexico is now having to take some of its own medicine, although Guatemala would never grant sanctuary to Zapatista leaders. On the contrary, the Mexican President and I have talked several times about the possibility of carrying out joint operations to prevent human traffic and arms contraband between our countries and make our borderline safer.

An area of social and economic development will be established along the border with several objectives. To prevent arms smuggling and the passage of armed individuals from one country to the other. To preclude the contraband of timber and archeological pieces. And to fight organized crime and implement a bilateral agreement against drug-trafficking. This has been highly effective and has extended to subversive elements. Mexico is now familiar with the pain of dealing with guerrillas. It cannot continue to host the Guatemalan guerrillas and will eventually have to set a deadline to resolve the problem.

All of this adds pressure to the guerrillas in our peace negotiations. They know it. What would happen if Mexico were to tell them, "You have two months to move out of the country; otherwise, we'll deport you." At that moment, with the closed-door agreement we have in Central America, they would have no choice but flee to some place in Europe. And that's very far. Transatlantic guerrillas would be more complicated, wouldn't they?

12

Economics with a Human Face

Question: *One of the accords with the guerrillas is to set up a Truth Commission. Aren't you afraid that, with all the brutal acts committed, blood may be found in the hands of many important figures?*

Ramiro de León Carpio: Yes, but there has been enough wisdom and maturity to avoid judicial effects. A lot has been said of the Truth Commission. Even the name has been an issue, for the official name is Historic Clarification Commission.

Its history dates back to the time when as Human Rights Commissioner I tried to set up this commission. Afterward, the National Center Union (UCN) party, based on the principles of forgiving and forgetting and of national reconciliation, supported the idea.

The forgetting element was put aside, for it was difficult to forget on both sides. I cannot ask the widow and orphan children of an officer killed to forget. To forgive, perhaps; to be part of a national reconciliation, maybe. But forgetting would be difficult. The same applies to the widow of a disappeared or murdered husband. So let's talk about forgiveness and national reconciliation. There was some reaction when I originally launched the proposal. There were groups claiming the disappeared. Finally, people have realized there's no use scratching a wound. Digging into the past is fine, if it's done with the purpose of reconciliation. But if it will create more problems, what's the use? I remember once telling myself, "Okay, I'll forgive, but I want to know whom I'm forgiving."

To seek forgiveness should be the mission of the Truth Commission, deciding and pointing at those to be forgiven. This has prompted intensive debate in Guatemala because the situation has lasted 34 years. In El Salvador there were only 10 years; more intense, but 10 years. In Guatemala many people have been involved, and this goes beyond the military and the guerrillas. Churches have been involved, especially the Catholic Church. At some point there were many priests and nuns involved in the guerrillas. And the church itself as an institution. It would be good now to know of the many diplomats and countries that were heavily involved.

Q: *A lot of controversy could come out of all this, with many accounts to settle.*

RDLC: Yes. This can be tremendously conflictive. That's what I mean when I say that in 34 years everyone has been somewhat involved. For example, we have had ambassadors directly participating. When the time comes to establish the truth, it would not suffice to point at the military officer or the guerrilla commander. What about the participation of this or that ambassador on a certain occasion in which there were such and such deaths? The nation is ultimately responsible.

Q: *Please be more specific. What countries are you referring to?*

RDLC: I would only say there's been a little of everything here. Not only Americans but Europeans as well. This has been a hotly debated issue. Yes, there's a sense of forgiveness so long as people know whom they are forgiving. All for the sake of durable peace and reconciliation.

It's hard. Cruel to those who have personally and directly suffered. It's easy for me to speak of reconciliation and forgiveness, but what about the widow or orphan children of the officer killed in a terrorist ambush, or of the husband and father executed extrajudicially by government forces? What of the mother of the kid blown up by a bomb he picked up believing the package was food. She's not going to want to forget, forgive or reconcile with the person who killed her loved one, be it a guerrilla, by accident, or whatever. It won't be easy for the thousands directly affected. Yet we need to work on this difficult task. It's a key element of the National Peace Plan I proposed.

Q: *How should the Truth Commission operate?*

RDLC: The truth of what happened on both sides is already known. It has been studied, investigated, analyzed. Wars are wars, and all wars are dirty. What needs to be done is to make the truth official. Confirm what is already known and reach a conclusion, always with the objective of strengthening the peace process. The Commission would have to look not only into what the army did, but also into what the guerrillas did. For example, who murdered German Ambassador Count William Von Spretti, or U.S. Ambassador John Gordon Mein and so many others. It's an endless story. It would be interesting for the guerrillas to know what happened on both sides.

This is why it was agreed that the Commission should not include the words Truth or Past in its name. Its official name is Historic Clarification and its purpose is to know and clarify all that happened at a particular time in our institutional and political life, so that by remembering it we avoid repeating it.

This is about strengthening reconciliation. It has no judicial consequences. It is simply to have a record of what happened. To clarify human rights violations and violent acts that have caused pain and suffering to Guatemalan people so that these sad events of our history are never repeated and our democratic process is strengthened.

Q: *Who would be part of the Commission?*

RDLC: The Commission will have three members: 1) The present moderator of the peace negotiations; 2) A citizen of irreproachable conduct, designated by the moderator with the consent of both sides; 3) An academician elected by the moderator with the consent of both sides from a list of three candidates submitted by the university presidents.

Q: *With so many difficulties ahead, you remain optimistic. Do you still believe peace is possible in Guatemala?*

RDLC: I'm totally optimistic. To say that conditions are not in place is not a valid argument. Of course there's poverty, misery, exploitation, injustice. That's what we want to resolve afterward. Had these issues been resolved, our country would be paradise and we would have no problems. If we opted to wait until the situation was perfect, we would have to wait quite a few years.

So I'm optimistic. There's international pressure as well as awareness that our government is willing. That's the big hope.

On the other hand, Guatemalans are becoming anxious and impatient. They are fed up and are beginning to express their desire that a peace treaty be signed. It adds to my optimism. Of course, absent the willpower, any excuse could be found to drop the issue. Anything socially compulsive — a strike, anything — would stop the process. For the guerrillas any excuse would do because they don't know what's going to happen politically. They don't know whether they'll gain anything by participating. There's a lot of uncertainty and those are my fears. I don't know whether the guerrillas will embrace the chance to incorporate into the political life of the country or if their strategy would be to wait and see and attempt to create a social base with the Indians. If they decide not to go along with the process, they will find an excuse. I will then have no alternative but to say I did my best effort and, since a peace agreement was not signed, I will pursue other means to address the issue.

But, again, I must be optimistic. More and more guerrillas are surrendering every day, meaning they have less in combat. I believe we are close to peace, and that will allow us to address the social issues we need to resolve.

We have many economic problems in Guatemala although in appearance Guatemala's economy is healthy. Our macroeconomics is favorable from the inflationary standpoint. Our monetary reserves, currency exchange and credit standing are stable. We have a very small external debt, and our economic growth is high. Yet poverty is a huge problem, and wealth is highly concentrated in very few hands.

Q: *Regardless of whether a peace agreement is signed or not, what are your economic priorities? How will you address the economic issues?*

RDLC: First, I must again say I found a crisis when I reached the presidency. Especially in the fiscal area. A tax reform had been implemented two years back in agreement with the private sector, but the results at the time I took office had been totally negative. Tax reforms are usually agreed to by the private sector and Congress. Because a structural reform has never been possible, tax reforms are tried every so often.

I found drained resources and huge debts. Only in hospitals, for example, I found an enormous debt of more than 130 million quetzals (approximately $32.5 million). The same in all other areas, all other ministries. This of course limits what can be devoted to social investments. I thus took a series of general economic measures, and established certain monetary, currency exchange and credit policies. By 1994 the results in economic variables were positive. The gross internal product, for example, yielded a growth of 4 percent for 1994, more than in 1993 and above the rate of population growth. This represents an increment in per-capita income.

In the monetary field, for example, we adopted measures to make currency exchange more flexible, which allowed us by 1994 to have better control of our hard currency without the Central Bank having to purchase the hard currency that entered the country. This resulted in the stability of the exchange rate. The national currency was not devalued and the quetzal remained in 1994 at the same level as 1993. Maintaining a monetary stability led to more guarantees and security.

Inflation kept a moderate trend during 1994, reaching 12 percent. It should have remained at 9 percent, but the general situation made it impossible. True, we have gone through a crisis, but we have addressed it with measures of austerity in spending. For the year 1995 the trend points at an inflation of 8 percent. Our final deficit would be barely 1.5 percent and we will cut it even more.

In spite of our financial crisis, the Bank of Guatemala has considerably reduced our external debt in $152 million. All this with a totally opposing Congress which did not permit us to approve many things. Even so, debt was reduced and it is estimated that in 1995 it will be $444 million. The external debt of $2 billion is one of the lowest in Latin America.

Finally, in the fiscal area, which is of utmost importance, the main challenge we found was that taxable revenue — especially taxes on income and added value — had dramatically diminished due to the government's serious financial problems. As I mentioned before, the tax reform carried out two years before by the private sector under President Serrano lowered the income-tax's highest rate of 34 percent to 25 percent, resulting in a depressed tax revenue. In Guatemala only 5 percent of the population pay taxes while 84 percent of the population live in poverty. It should be all the way around, 84 percent paying taxes and only 5 percent living in poverty. This should be our goal, the ideal we should aim at and fight for.

The reduced tax revenue led to a considerable deficit in 1994. On the other hand, a ruling by the Constitutional Court slowed us down in early 1994. In an incredibly political ruling, we were no longer permitted to collect taxes in advance, which was standard procedure in Guatemala. Although the court's ruling was appealed on grounds of unconstitutionality, we failed to collect much revenue. This, compounded by the tax-rate reduction prompted by the tax reform, led to a deficit.

Q: *You failed to collect how much, about $200 million?*

RDLC: Yes, approximately $200 million. In addition, we began our presidential term with a huge scandalous debt inherited from our predecessor. Since we had less revenue to deal with a high level of spending, we had to resort to financing through a bond issue. Notwithstanding these adverse conditions, my government, acting on principles of absolute honesty, transparence and austerity, complied with the amortization program of the debt established with the Bank of Guatemala, and carried out a social investment of 76 percent, which is an unprecedented level in the history of Guatemala.

We thus embarked on a tax reform, which by changing the structure would yield fruits to Guatemalan future governments. This was important and highly positive.

Q: *What makes this reform different from the many other tax reforms executed in Guatemala?*

RDLC: Ours was not a cosmetic or circumstantial tax reform, but one with depth and accompanied by an administrative reform based on three principles: 1) make tax payments easy; bureaucratic hurdles have made contributions cumbersome; 2) make collection efficient; and 3) develop a penalty system to punish those who evade taxes.

There's a culture of evasion here. In Guatemala taxes are paid at the rates established by the company's accountant. There's this notion that the government steals and wastes rather than invests, which has been the argument for evading taxes. At this moment, however, this is a false premise because it has been proven that this government makes honest use of tax proceeds — on highways, water supplies, services.

Q: *Hasn't a proposal to make everyone pay his share caused you major problems?*

RDLC: There was always open dialogue and, specifically in 1994, I opened a debate with all segments of the Guatemalan society, fundamentally with the business sector, to present my first proposal. The Finance Ministry and my economic team had submitted a number of options to me and, after conscious analysis, I chose one and presented it as a basic scenario. I then asked for observations or opposing points for revision.

The business sector did not offer alternatives. These were people used to having their way on economic issues. Before, all it took was a phone call to the minister or even the President. I guess they resented my saying publicly that the business sector had been involved in corruption before, in cash-in-the-briefcase kind of operations. It must have hurt them.

The situation now is different. I can attest that in Guatemala the high-ranking finance officials under my presidency are people of absolute honesty, who do not accept pressure, bribes or deals of any nature.

Businessmen were confident they had a new Congress — a very good one, by the way — and believed I would never persuade Congressmen to confront the business sector. They were wrong in not offering me a counter-proposal. They were conscious that the country needed a tax reform, that the government needed the revenue to guarantee macro-economic growth, and that I needed their help. In fact, shortly before presenting the reforms to Congress, some of my friends approached me asking how much I needed for my budget. One billion? We can give you two billion, they said, to cover your budget. The offer was tempting, because with that kind of money I could have carried out my program. Yet, I told them: "You keep looking at things short-term, and though I'm interested in covering my budget, I'm even more interested in establishing the foundation for a flow of revenue that would help the nation, lest the next president encounter a similar situation." He would be taking office in January of 1996 in need of another circumstantial reform which will no longer be an option. And that's the bottom line. I told party leaders that to start another reform in January 1996 would delay social accomplishments one or two years, and in that period the whole situation could blow up.

On the other hand, if we now embark on a good reform — and I showed them charts — when the new president takes office in January 1996 everything would be under control. All that would be needed is to collect efficiently and any social outburst could be addressed normally. The business sector didn't understand this. They just believed the bill would not pass and, even worse — and this is what really bothered me — they didn't even give me a response or a counter-offer.

Under the circumstances, I ended my dialogue with the business sector and began a dialogue with Congress. By the way, I was able to sense the improvement resulting from the Congressional purge. This was now a modest, patriotic Congress, with a clear political vision of Guatemala's future. I convinced its members with technical, financial and political arguments. The issue was not to carry out a biased allocation of resources nor to give out money directly to Congressmen in the corrupt style of the past. Tax legislation was finally approved, including an income-tax increase from 25 to 30 percent; the elimination of privileges and tax exemptions; a 1.5 percent tax on fixed assets of corporations, a mechanism that has worked well in other countries as a complement of income tax. If tomorrow tax collection reaches a normal level, perhaps the income-tax rate could be lowered, or the complement tax could decrease.

Here's the way it would work. A businessman who should be paying 100 evades tax and pays only 10 or nothing. With this tax he will pay at least 80, which is then credited to income tax. He who is complying loses nothing because he is making his contribution. This guarantees immediate funds when necessary.

Another change approved was the increase of Added Value Tax (IVA) from 7 to 10 percent, provided the three-point increment, which is to be invested in the rural areas of the country, become effective when the peace treaty is signed on January 1, 1996.

This sums up our tax reform. The only other issue was the creation of a penalty system in view of the country's history of tax evasion. Congress established the category of tax crime and set up tax courts with a system of fines and sanctions, business closures and jail time for violators. This paved the way to normal resources and an investment budget for the next government.

We have also made reforms in other areas. For example, there has been abuse of tax credits and deductions granted on many imports, such as yachts, planes, vehicles, jewelry, trips to Europe, etc. This was not right, and when I told businessmen, they agreed.

There was an enterprise that donated 30,000 or 40,000 quetzals (approximately $7,500 or $10,000) to the Social Welfare Office, where my wife worked. So she came to me one day and said that with our new tax she would no longer receive funds for their homeless children. I investigated the matter and, indeed, this enterprise donated money to my wife's social cause, which earned his owner an irregularly applied tax credit and exemption of other taxes. I approached him and told him: "Look, don't bother to donate more money and pay your taxes. This way you will help your society more."

It's not only a matter of legislation. We must change the mentality of this society and other reforms may be necessary for that.

Q: *But didn't the Constitutional Court pull off some trick and suspend part of the tax reform?*

RDLC: Right. Under political pressure from the powerful economic sector, the Constitutional Court again stood in the way of reaching my goals, this time economic. Let me tell you what has transpired since the very beginning and how I had to resort to a political measure — temporary, extraordinary — to exert pressure and save, if not all, at least a big part of the tax reform that was almost lost. This has been the most difficult battle I've had to fight during my administration. My first battle had been against the military factor, and the next one against the political factor. But this was against the economic factor, by far the toughest and most important of all. Achieving institutional/military and political stability would have been for naught had economic stability not been attained. These three elements of stability — institutional, political and economic — were indispensable to address the fourth: the social factor. And if the latter were to be neglected due to economic instability, the political element could be overturned and that, in turn, could lead to institutional instability and a backward effect.

As a constitutional lawyer I can affirm that the laws contained in our tax reform package were not unconstitutional, as the business sector tried to prove. On the contrary, the purpose of this tax reform was to achieve the fundamental government's goal of combating poverty through public investment and social spending.

Our financial performance over the first four months of the 1995 demonstrated that it was a worthwhile effort. We surpassed the revenue budget in more than 130 million quetzals (approximately $32.5 million), and 324 million quetzals (approximately $81 million) over the preceding year. Furthermore, the International Monetary Fund has announced the upcoming approval of the Shadow Accord, which will support our economic program and will allow us to present it in Paris before the international community in an effort to gather financial support for our peace programs.

Q: *But what did the court actually do?*

RDLC: Responding to claims of unconstitutionality presented before it, the Constitutional Court temporarily suspended two important articles of the Income Tax Law affecting the flow of government's resources for the present year. Faced with such ruling, I adopted, with the President of Congress and the secretaries of political parties, measures to absorb the impact of the temporary suspension.

It became necessary to temporarily abandon the custom tariff component of our foreign trade policy in favor of adopting, as an emergency short-term measure, a unified tariff that would provide the government with the financial resources it needed while it tried to restore the articles suspended by the Constitutional Court. Additionally, we tried to find a legislative alternative toward a permanent revenue in line with the initial purpose of our tax reform. Of course, such measure shook up the business sector, particularly its industrial and agricultural segments, and it almost prompted a more serious confrontation.

Two bills were passed as a result of our initiative to fight back after the high court's suspension. One of them, the Law for Taxing Financial Products, completely restored the revenue suspended by the court. The other one, the Law for Taxing Commercial and Agricultural Enterprises, restored the contribution by commercial entities. They were both approved as national emergency measures after a final agreement by the Executive and Legislative branches of government with the private sector. They will help diminish the impact of the suspended articles of our Income Tax Law.

Notwithstanding the hurdles we have had to overcome, our Tax Reform will have positive results for the nation, and the political cost of its defense will be compensated by the benefits that Guatemala will reap in the future. However, we need to continue our struggle for a tax morality to which all Guatemalans may feel committed.

Q: *And what happened to the political measures you had to take? Did you have to back out?*

RDLC: No. It allowed me to retake control of the economic policy, especially in the area of foreign trade. The temporary unified tariff was later annulled within the framework of the safeguard clause of the Central American custom tariff system, which allows a government to take these types of measures unilaterally without violating Central American treaties. The political measures had accomplished their purpose of partially restoring what was suspended by the court. Since the strategy worked, there was no reason to leave the measures in effect.

It is evident that a fiscal improvement paves the way to

lower tariffs, which is the goal of Central American countries, to be attained gradually.

I also asked Congress to approve — and it finally did — the final act incorporating the results of the Uruguay Round of the multilateral trade negotiations sponsored by the world trade organization. This will allow the implementation of tariffs consolidated by GATT, which protect agricultural products affected by market distortions and disloyal competition.

After our dialogue leading to the agreement on alternative revenue legislation, the private sector committed itself to support the Tax Reform and to abide by the law. Further, they agreed to help develop an immediate tax-morality campaign to encourage a tax-payer's conscience.

Moving toward political and economic stability, a government is called to respond to the biggest challenge for mankind — social care as it fights poverty and injustice.

Q: *After the confrontation with the business sector and the political agreement, what were the specific accomplishments of the Tax Reform?*

RDLC: The Tax Reform can generate additional revenue of as much as 1,678 million quetzals (approximately $419.5 million), broken down as shown in this spreadsheet that you may want to share with your readers.*

The Tax Reform will have an impact on 1996. For 1995, however, there's still a financial gap to overcome, and Congress is pondering the possibility of creating an extraordinary tax to avoid a large deficit for next year, as well as keeping a close watch on public spending.

The resulting increment will allow the next government to manage improved levels of investment and social expense, which is the whole purpose of the reform. The amounts apportioned for investment, not including social spending (health and education), was Q2,200 million (approximately $550 million) in 1995, to which must be added an impact of

---

** Please see Income Tax Table in Appendix A.*

Q1,678 million (approximately $419.5 million) for 1996, for a total of Q3,878 million (approximately $969.5 million) guaranteed for the next government to invest on social needs and fight poverty without needing to negotiate a tax reform.

As far as administrative measures, the increment reported by the Public Finance Ministry for the first four months of 1995 reflects the application of administrative measures, such as the audit of custom services and opening them for bids as part of a semi-privatization program. The revenue increment was Q130 million (approximately $32.5 million) over what was budgeted for that period in 1995 and Q324 million (approximately $81 million) over the first four months of the preceding year. This means that the Tax Reform is yielding fruit, considering that at the end of the previous year tax revenues were declining. Our objective was to halt that decline and improve revenue behavior in a way to spark the positive trend it's already accomplishing.

Q: *Did your personal relations with the major businessmen end up under a bad light after this reform?*

RDLC: Not at all. A politician not willing to dialogue and compromise is not the good politician a president is expected to be.

The conversations have been resumed on 20 more topics besides taxes. There was a confrontation, but by acting timely and decisively we prevented it from becoming a major war. They bought full-page ads in the newspapers opposing the reform. I never uttered a word in response. Not one. It was a strong attack, but the truth is there is great mutual respect and a good relationship. They acknowledge there is honesty and good intentions in my work. After serious discrepancies and not reaching agreement on all items, we are now again sitting at the table debating other topics in the national agenda, such as peace, citizen security, etc.

Q: *Privatization is an important issue. What is the balance of your efforts in that area? How do you feel about the criticism for approaching it at such a slow pace?*

RDLC: Let me begin by saying that this issue was on the

government's agenda for the years 1994 and 1995. Never before a president has made reference to the issue of privatization for fear of losing an election, which is obviously not my case. Since I have no electoral objectives and therefore have no worry over political cost, I have done things other presidents could never dream of doing. I have announced, for instance, that we will act against monopolies in general and will privatize all pertinent state-run enterprises.

Privatization, which is an essential part of decentralization, is not something I have pulled out of my sleeve at the last moment. It's included in the government plan for 1994-95. I even appointed Dr. Manuel Ayau Cordón — knowledgeable, honest, the best person for the job — to head the Privatization Commission.

Of course, there have been problems. All privatization effort must follow certain rules. One is to set the scene and promote the issue with widespread information bound to persuade the public, the consumer and union leaders. This is what we have been lacking. I have thrown my full support behind the issue and we are at a stage of consultation.

Q: *Does this mean to allow competition, for example, in the area of telephone and electricity services?*

RDLC: Right. In the area of electricity, to eliminate monopoly. In the area of telephones, first to eliminate monopoly and then privatization. In transportation, the workers of Railroad of Guatemala (FEGUA) are totally in agreement. It will have positive results, not only from its sale and privatization of service, but for the impact on the oil pipeline, the optical cable, and the dry channel from one ocean to the other.

Privatization is an urgent matter. Certain property and facilities to be privatized lose value by the day due to technological advantages of the competition. In five or six years they may not be worth anything. In other words, unless they are privatized they will destroy by themselves. We either privatize or establish the foundation for the future to take advantage of the added effect on a lower inflation rate. The resulting revenue from privatization will be devoted to amortize debts of the Bank of Guatemala.

Q: *Are you not afraid of a strong protest from unions? How willing are you to face it and endure it?*

RDLC: Shortly after I took office the entire public sector went on a strike that lasted 11 weeks. At the end, the unions finally gave in because I held my ground and did not make concessions that we couldn't make. What they were demanding was unreal and they lacked enough participation. It was practically a defeat that has placed them in a weak position afterward.

I sincerely trust their inability to summon enough members from their ranks and the government's capacity to hold its ground on an issue that will benefit the people.

Q: *A significant part of Guatemalan economy, estimated at approximately three-fifths, depends on agriculture and cattle-breeding. The nation's economy needs to diversify.*

RDLC: I believe Guatemala has a lot of potential once it resolves its political problems. One of them is the nation's democratization. On this we feel reassured. Had you asked this question 15 years ago I would have talked about electoral fraud, absence of democracy, and too many authoritarian governments. Now we have substantial political stability and democracy is a reality beyond any doubt.

The second problem is signing a peace treaty. If we accomplish this, the country will gain enormous credibility, which will allow us to devote our time to improve productivity and modernize our institutions. We have before us, if not an industrialization program, a semi-industrialization effort and a competitive position in certain non-traditional products. In the first four months of 1995 we have had a 63 percent increment in exports of non-traditional products as compared with 1994, and tourism has doubled. The indigenous communities living on high regions of the country can produce fruits, vegetables, flowers, all goods for which we have a huge open market in the United States, Canada, Mexico, with whom we intend to subscribe a free-trade agreement. All these indigenous communities need is financial aid, technical assistance and help in marketing their products.

Another field of great potential is tourism. Once the country is politically stabilized, once peace becomes a reality, the nation will have resources to apply to the infrastructure. Highways, telephone systems and electrical lines will be there for tourism. In three years Guatemala's main source of revenue will be tourism, no doubt about it. It is my policy to fully support tourism. I truly believe it's where we can compete and we need to prepare ourselves from the vantage point of being the closest neighbor to the more powerful economic bloc in the world — NAFTA (North Atlantic Free Trade Agreement). I've referred to this geographical fact as both an advantage and a disadvantage. It's like being the neighbor of a very rich man, and if we ready ourselves, which is what our productive sector is doing, we could be part of this in an advantageous way.

Q: *These transformations you describe are to take place in a country, whose population has an indigenous majority. These indigenous communities have a very closed culture, based on subsistence. How to conform the indigenous world to the modernization processes?*

RDLC: That is, precisely, the great opportunity for the indigenous world to survive. In other words, because of their ancestors, their culture and tradition, many of these communities have limited themselves to merely subsist, living almost on barter transactions. Communities that produce carrots, for example, go to the market to exchange them for coffee. The reason for this is that they haven't had the opportunity to develop further, but this can change if they get a chance to improve their production. Improvement in size and flavor, for instance, will represent greater revenue, and then they will not only subsist but will have enough to take care of other expenses, such as clothes for their children, etc. They deserve such opportunity. These are people who love to work and trade, and can be helped easily.

I just visited a community with the president of a private bank, and he was impressed by an existing project for producing and exporting non-traditional products, such as ornamental flowers and plants. The organizational skills and the productivity of the indigenous community are incredible. All they need is a little bit of assistance. They are no longer thinking of merely subsisting, but are actually going beyond that point. This is fundamental.

This means that this kind of labor will no longer be employed in traditional tasks; they will no longer go down to the coast where sugar-cane planting, growing and cutting processes are being mechanized. They need less labor by the day, and those workers now remain in the high areas, which becomes a psychological, cultural and family advantage since they won't have to go all the way down far from their homes. The downward slope is risky and dangerous, workers have to separate from their families and be exposed to diseases and different customs, etc.

In other words, modernization is beneficial to the indigenous communities that are developing with much impetus, interest, hope and participation.

I'm bent on economic development, monetary stability, lower interest rates, lower inflation level, stronger currency reserves, payment of external and internal debt, etc. All of this creates an obligation to comply with existing treaties with international finance organizations, with whom we have, by the way, very good standing. They acknowledge our efforts. It all leads to economic development, which we are currently achieving and will continue to achieve and improve.

Economic development must have a human face, however. It must have a social face, lest only a few benefit from our growth. This has been the story of Guatemala and it's been of no use to anyone.

We need that sensitivity, the conscious determination to achieve economic development extensive to all popular segments of our society — peasants, workers, elderly people. This is the answer to the nation's problems. In a country where social needs — work, health, education, nutrition, housing — are satisfied, no one should have a reason to be unhappy. On the other hand, if there is discrimination and economic growth benefits only a few, and social needs are not met nor social services enjoyed by most, malcontent groups will emerge. We need benefits for all and not for just a few. In other words, if all human rights — economic, social and cultural — are respected in a society, it can attain peace and happiness.

What After Ramiro de León Carpio?

By Santiago Aroca

Months before the 1995 elections for the Guatemalan presidency, two names captured the voters' preference in the polls. One of them was Alvaro Arzú, former mayor of Guatemala City and candidate for the center-right National Advancement Party (*Partido de Avanzada Nacional*).

In the summer of 1995, Arzú scored a 30 percent preference in the polls and had all the possibilities of becoming the next democratic Guatemalan president. Politically, his candidacy represented continuity and stability. Committed to advance social-economic reforms further, Arzú also expressed a will to continue negotiating with the guerrillas toward a peaceful solution of the nation's 34-year civil war.

Surprisingly, only one other name shared the spotlight with Arzú in the 1995 summer polls — Gen. Efraín Ríos Montt, whose candidacy is banned by the Constitution, which expressly forbids any person who has taken part in a military coup d'etat to run for president.

Ríos Montt was the Congressman who had obtained more votes in the 1994 election, and his group, the Republican Front of Guatemala (*Frente Republicano de Guatemala*) obtained a majority of seats in Congress. Ríos Montt thus became the president of the Guatemalan Congress.

In the presidential elections 3.5 million people are eligible to vote. The electoral census is composed of exactly 3,350,840 voters, of which 1,161,314 are illiterate. It was to this segment of Guatemalan electoral population that Ríos Montt appealed with the promise of safety and justice in a country suffering its worst crime wave ever.

Ríos Montt seems undisturbed by the constitutional clause that bans his candidacy. "I don't care what the Constitution says," he told a group of foreign correspondents in the summer of 1995. "We live in a broken country, destroyed and looted, and I will do what it needs to be done to save it."

In 1982, after reaching power through a coup, Ríos Montt developed a policy of burned land against the leftist guerrillas. This gained him a reputation of being a ruthless ruler. In the Guatemalan conflict, in which 150,000 people have died, the "special courts," if not created by Ríos Montt they had nonetheless his strongest support, stood out for its cruelty.

A man of religious ways, Ríos Montt belonged to the Protestant church of the Resurrected Christ. The General used to appear on television every Sunday to read the bible. Many Indians remember him as a pious man who liberated them from the guerrilla threat. Also referred to as an honest person who did not loot the presidency, Ríos Montt did not flinch from asking that any officer taking money from the CIA.

The impediment to run for president unleashed an internal crisis in Ríos Montt's party that prompted the resignation of congressman and business man Arturo Soto, who had contributed funds to the political adventures of Ríos Montt. Soto was one of the possible replacements for Ríos Montt in FRG's electoral ticket, but he presented his resignation alleging that the party had moved away from its principles.

At the bottom of the FRG's crisis was Ríos Montt's decision to present the presidential candidacy of his wife María Teresa Sosa de Ríos. Hours after unsuccessfully appealing the constitutional precept before court, the party confirmed that Ríos Montt's wife would head the party's electoral ticket with congressman Harris Withbeck as the vice presidential candidate.

Even under the uncertainty surrounding its primary candidate in the summer of 1995, FRG topped all the polls over Arzú's National Advancement Party (Partido de Avanzada Nacional). Besides these two candidates there were approximately 15 presidential candidates registered. The better known among them were Mario Castejón, for Partido de los Descamisados (Shirtless Party) , and Gen. Hector Alejandro Gramajo, former Defense Minister (1986-1990), for Frente de Unidad Nacional (National Unity Front).

Guatemalan political mainstream parties are Democracia Cristiana (Christian Democrats), Union del Centro Nacional (National Unity Center) and Partido Socialista Democratico (Social Democrat Party). All three announced they are supporting former foreign affairs minister Fernando Andrade, advisor to president Kjell Laugerud (1974-1978) and main assessor of General Oscar Mejía, after the coup of 1983.

13

No Second Term, Thank You

Question: *Mr. President, a good part of your term has taken place with a Congress dominated by former dictator Efraín Ríos Montt. How do you regard the electoral triumph in parliamentary elections of Ríos Montt's Republican Front and the present protagonism of this figure emerged from a sinister past in Guatemala?*

Ramiro de León Carpio: After the Constitutional reform, in the legislative elections that followed, we attained an honest and clean Congress. The best proof is the approval of the Tax Reform package and other laws benefiting the nation.

That was a great step forward. Yet people only get the rulers they deserve because they elect them. Due to ignorance, lack of political conscience, absence of democratic education; for whatever reason, that's democracy. So a Congress is formed by two majority parties — one, the Guatemalan Republican Front (*Frente Republicano Guatemalteco, FRG*) led by Gen. Efraín Ríos Montt; the other, National Action Party (*Partido de Avanzada Nacional, PAN*) led by Alvaro

Arzú. The Republican Front has a strong though uncertain leadership.

Q: *How do you explain that leadership, the phenomenom of former dictator Ríos Montt's popularity?*

RDLC: The phenomenom can be explained by an eagerness of order, of security. Gen. Ríos Montt projects tranquility. A very strange personality, the general imparts confidence, strength, energy, sometimes excessive. He has already shown his authoritarianism. As de facto Chief of State he created special tribunals which could give a death sentence to whomever they wished. These were secret courts, top secret, accused of many human rights violations. On the first day after he became de facto Chief of State, there was absolute calmness. During the first few months, the crime problem was resolved. But it was all momentary, psychological. Little by little it reappeared, and there was as much or more anarchy than before he had assumed power. In other words, the idea people have of him is somewhat fallacious, deceptive.

People want someone with a sense of order, they yearn for Gen. Ubico. They wished Gen. Ubico could come back to resolve the violence problem, but they forget that his was another era, when Guatemala was a tiny silver cup and he was a dictator. Right now, under a democratic system, I doubt even Gen. Ubico could resolve that problem.

I believe Ríos Montt's popularity is diluting. He was more before; today he is less. For example, the fact that we let the people elect their representatives democratically was a great lesson. They learned that effective mechanisms do exist, and that there's no need to use the stick, break the law, or act violently to resolve things. They have learned these lessons gradually. People are now aware that democracy is better than dictatorship, and they took to the streets to defend democracy from Serrano's *coup d'etat*. This means it's not absolutely true that the entire population supports Ríos Montt. Some see him as a savior; yet if — and this is my own personal opinion — Gen. Ríos Montt were to run for president, who knows how he would fare. Many would fear his reactions, and many would unite in a common front, maybe not to vote for someone but to vote against Gen. Ríos Montt. I have my doubts, and I'd be inclined to think he would not win. The truth is, nonetheless, that he has leadership for the reasons I've mentioned. This would have been inconceivable in Europe or in the United States. How could people want someone like Ríos Montt, a dictator and a human rights violator?

Q: *In Guatemala voices have been raised indicating the Constitution forbids a person with Ríos Montt's background to participate in politics. What is your opinion?*

RDLC: To me the norm is very clear as to what is required to be a presidential candidate. The Constitution says that candidates who have participated in a *coup d'etat* or have become chief of state by means of a *coup d'etat*, cannot opt to run for president. The wording is clear: not only does it specify such person can't become president, but clearly forbids him from even being a candidate.

Besides, the Constitution establishes in his Article 46 that, in human rights issues, international treaties and conventions ratified by Guatemala would bear preeminence over domestic legislation. There are various things here: first, domestic legislation contained in the Constitution actually forbids him being a candidate; further, the Constitutional Court has also officially said no; and there have been pronouncements within the framework of international law opposing such candidacy. In fact, there's a specific ruling from the Inter-American Human Rights Court that he cannot be a presidential candidate.

Q: *What would be the impact on Guatemala if Ríos Montt were to become president of Guatemala?*

RDLC: He cannot be a candidate. Unless the constitutional norm is modified, he will not be president of this country, and it's too late to make amendments before the next election. So it's actually a moot point. Nevertheless, based on such hypothesis, I will give you my opinion about the impact it would have, both nationally and internationally.

Nationally, if there were no legal impediment and people elected him, we would have a president whose expectations to resolve the security problem would vanish in the first few months. If he was not able to resolve it under a dictatorial regime with all the military force at his call, much less would he be able to resolve it under a democratic system. There's even one more peril. The military relieved him of the highest post for creating instability within their institution. He was a great officer, but he acted against military hierarchy and order. Would he behave the same way again in this situation? We don't know, but he is considered to be a threat to the stability of an institution, which today is totally stable.

Internationally, the impact would be totally negative. I know of countries which would possibly withdraw their diplomatic representations. International aid would be highly conditioned, at least at the beginning, with a wait-and-see attitude. In other words, we would go backwards 20 years, and these are not my words but the feeling of the international community. It would be negative to Guatemala and its peace process.

Q: *Ríos Montt is a religious fanatic. How do you explain the tremendous growth of evangelical churches in Guatemala?*

RDLC: Indeed, religious sects of all kinds have launched an offensive throughout Latin America. Very diverse sects. In general, the Evangelical Church has had a big offensive with — and I say this very seriously — very positive evangelizing mission. While the Catholic Church has rested in its laurels, the Evangelical Church has spread its temples in big numbers throughout the country. Catholicism is still deeply rooted and has not been surpassed in Guatemala, but it has weakened. It carries out little evangelizing work, and does not do much pastoral missionary work. I'm not saying Catholics don't do it, but not enough. Now that they are relegated, frightened and worried, they have tried other strategies, although rather late. This is criticism I direct to my own church. I am a Catholic, and long before becoming President, I told Catholic bishops that the church lacks the missionary spirit that's needed now. They have failed in that respect and others have defeated them, as it happens in any activity.

I don't think Ríos Montt can be associated with the success of the Evangelical Church. My predecessor, Jorge Serrano Elías, was an evangelical, and it came a point when the Guatemalan Evangelical Church opposed him. Despite being apolitical, the church will not give its unconditional support to any candidate or new president. It could like this or that candidate better, but I don't give it much importance.

There is competition between Catholics and Evangelists. The Catholic Church must strengthen its apostolate. It's doing it through its lay members and, in that sense, it shouldn't be considered a war. Contrary to such belief, I think there will come a time in which a unification of all Christians will take place because the last thing Guatemala needs is a religious war.

Q: *Will you take someone's side in the upcoming elections? Will you support a candidate?*

RDLC: Not at all. I will remain absolutely neutral, not only as a president but as government. No government resources will be used. That's one of the advantages of not having a political party. This way I strengthen the electoral purity and avoid attacks. There will be no reason to attack me.

Q: *Please respond sincerely. Would you like to have a longer term?*

RDLC: No. I accepted the challenge knowing it was going to be hard and short, that time would go quickly. It was only half a term and I am pleased to have accomplished things not previously achieved in a full term. But my mission ends there. I believe in political moments, and this one was for becoming president. Many people feel I should have waited and taken a shot at a full term through elections. It was a possibility.

I chose to get here without compromises, owing nothing to the military, the business, political, religious sectors – nobody. There was no time to make deals nor would I have accepted them. I arrived in total freedom and that's something that gives me great satisfaction. On the other hand, if I had made it to the presidency through the other road, who knows. For example, I couldn't have eliminated the millionaire confidential funds and other things in one stroke of my pen. Yes, I believe in political moments and my moment came then and ends on January 14, 1996. History is judging me, whether I did good, bad or just so-so. People are judging me, and I'll leave with the satisfaction of having done what I had to do within my possibilities. That's the art of politics — the art of what's possible, not of what's not.

Q: *Have you not been tempted to use the mechanisms the Constitution places at your disposal to run for a second presidential term?*

RDLC: No, for two reasons. First, it would amount to deceiving the people. I accepted the commitment for two and a half years and I cannot be so irresponsible as to resign before the end of the term to opt for another term.

The other reason is that I have no party nor political structure. There are the traditional parties and Ríos Montt's front. Christian Democrats are not doing well. It's in decline because it's a hinge party, turning to one side or another in its decisions.

As to my former party, the National Center Union (UCN), there are a few fresh faces, but the panorama is not very good. I think it is a party that could renovate its cadres completely and make an attempt, albeit with difficulty, considering it is charged with the grave historical responsibility of all we are suffering now and the golden opportunity it wasted.

UCN has a big atomization problem and it wasn't doing well even with Jorge Carpio's presence. An atomized party joined by people who, in my opinion, never should have joined and who not only gave the party a bad name, but wanted to steal it away, people who fought Jorge Carpio before and keep feuding with remaining members. The party was agonizing and will participate in the elections possibly in coalition with another party. If it has the vision of reaching an alliance with the winning party, it will obtain some Congressional seats, 10 at the maximum, and some quota of power, a ministry perhaps, merely to survive. It would find it difficult to renovate. I believe it's history. I think it fulfilled a really important historic mission, but it's finished, pretty much like the UCD in Spain, which lived through the transition into democracy and ended its mission.

Q: *So you totally dismiss running for a new presidential term?*

RDLC: For now I emphatically dismiss it. I am no longer interested in any constitutional reform or any other issue that would prompt me to submit my candidacy in the next election. I am reaching a new period in my life. I'll devote my time to writing, reflection. There are many other things I want to do.

Q: *Are you going to write your memoirs?*

RDLC: Of course. I have always written and now feel moved to write some things I have pending. I wish to combine my experience as commissioner and President and write about it. Perhaps I can make a contribution to the country, to future presidents.

It has been difficult. It's been hard in many ways, but it has been gratifying. I have enjoyed the political chess game, especially the accomplishments and the goals reached. Yet I have paid a high price, from the personal and family standpoints. My wife, our children, the family as a whole has had to pay a high price. Colombian former President Belisario Betancourt has written about what others believe is the honey of power. He referred to suffering in power as the "penalties of power."

Q: *Do you like power?*

RDLC: Yes, if it is to achieve goals and help the people. This is where I find the greatest satisfaction, to be able to solve people's problems. It fascinates me and I truly enjoy that type of power.

Three months after taking office, when I embarked in the purge and was greeted by the people and heard their clamor throughout my nationwide tour, I remember I telephoned my wife and told her: "Look, I received my pay today." Three months had gone by and of course I had received my compensation in money for that period. But she asked: "What do you mean? You hadn't been paid?" She had not understood. So I told her: "It's that I truly earned my salary today. I received the great satisfaction of the Guatemalan people, and that is compensation at its best." There's no greater joy than to receive the support of the people. It's not a tangible pay but it's delicious. The other kind does not interest me. In fact, I lost my first check. I don't know what I did with it; they had to issue a new one.

What I can assure you is that I do not admire power for power's sake. Mexican writer Carlos Fuentes said it best when he said that "the empire of violence is infinite. Only three pieces of advice can dispel it: Never admire power, never hate your enemy, and never scorn those who suffer."

Jurist and diplomat Alejandro Maldonado Aguirre made a reference to me in relation to Fuentes's three pieces of advice:

"a) As to 'never admire power,' De León Carpio did not pursue power for power's sake. He reached it as a natural consequence of Guatemala's yearning for a constitutional solution to a political crisis.

"De León Carpio did not need to campaign nor compromise with any power segment, be it political, economic or military.

"His government promoted initiatives of constitutional reform with the purpose of purifying sectors of government that had fallen prey to corruption of power and of judicial bias. Impartial systems were designed for appointing high officials in charge of controlling power and public funds. He discarded the possibility of managing 'confidential' funds that were a source of corruption and abuse of executive jurisdiction. No 'official' party was organized or installed, and his government maintains the most absolute neutrality vis-a-vis the electoral process to be opened soon. In other words, the President has no intention of keeping quotas of power for the future. He turned down the suggestion made by various sectors to try to exercise a second term.

"b) Regarding the advice 'never hate your enemy,' De

León Carpio energized the peace initiative and gave consistency to the negotiating process. The government subscribed agreements that represented an advance in negotiations with guerrillas grouped under the URNG, and has maintained the flexibility and realism necessary to reach a fair and durable peace accord that would not humiliate anybody.

"c) And, finally, to 'never scorn those who suffer,' De León Carpio has made the fight against poverty the focal point of his government policy. Also tax reform, intentional redistribution, and the possibility of obtaining resources for programs to achieve integral development for the individual and the nation."

14

The Mechanisms of Power

Question: *How much money does the President of Guatemala make?*
Ramiro de León Carpio: By law, the President makes about 40,000 quetzals annually (approximately $10,000). It's a really low salary, but of course all his expenses are paid for.
Q: *Don't you currently have any other source of income?*
RDLC: No, except the properties I had before becoming President and my personal savings. It's sufficient because I hardly have expenses to pay. The President's expenses — travels, meals, everything — are paid for by the government. Otherwise, I couldn't have lived on that low salary, considerably lower than what I made in my private professional practice. The presidential salary could be kept low because it didn't really matter. The President had access to 50, 60, 100 million quetzals (approximately $12.5, $15, $25 million) of confidential funds that he could use at his discretion, and the salary in itself was merely symbolic. We kept it at the same level,

raising only the funds for expenses.

Q: *What virtues are needed to be President?*

RDLC: Virtues? I'd say the first one should be honesty. Also wisdom, and all the humbleness and modesty you can muster. The ability to listen, for which I've been highly criticized, and patience, a lot of patience and tolerance. But, in the end, perhaps the most important is the strength to make decisions.

Q: *You've been criticized for listening too much.*

RDLC: Yes. I've been called indecisive because I consult with others. If you analyze the goals I set for myself, all of them have been getting done. The road I chose was slow and long, which was perhaps the road some did not want, but results is what counts, not the procedure or the mechanism used.

I insist the most important quality in a leader is his honesty. If he has no honesty, and also transparence and a sense of austerity, the people immediately reject him. Especially in a country as poor as ours. The president of a poor country must represent his nation as it really is and in no other way.

I'm proud to be the President of a courageous nation, noble, sacrificed, stoic, with a high sense of honor, but very poor. In other words, I can't afford to incite luxuries that would hurt the population, like some of my predecessors who have incurred in unfortunate extravagance. I just can't. In my government there has been tremendous austerity, exaggerated sometimes in its transparence and honesty, the very qualities required of a president.

Q: *You said you were proud to be the president of a poor country. When you are with presidents of powerful countries like the United States or a European nation, what do you feel? Do you feel you're representing a lesser country in front of the powerful and great?*

RDLC: Not at all. The greatest value a nation can have is its national identity, and I am proud to represent a population with a culture that surpasses in thousands of years that of some of the countries mentioned, a nation in the rise, with values and history. It's truly gratifying. On the contrary, when I am with other presidents of powerful countries, I feel even better.

Q: *Whom do you listen to? Who surrounds you, whom do you trust?*
RDLC: All my life I've followed a system of organized disorder. That's why I need a staff capable of establishing some order around me, and these people are very important to me. I've always been a good listener. I listen to various people although in the end I make the decisions, at times contrary to the advice given me, especially on political issues.

I am a person with many advisers. Here, there, inside, outside, and it all depends on the issue and the circumstance. There are important players in the government, of course, I can't deny it. They're all important as a team, but there are some whom I blindly trust for their honesty and knowledge, and for their loyalty to me. These I can count with the fingers of one hand, and this is not to say the rest is no good. Only that I trust them and consult with them, though at times they can be wrong and I pay no attention to their advice. Maybe three, four, five people, depending on the issue; a couple of them on any issue of government. These are people who cover my back, who are loyal, patriotic and honest, and whose solid principles and professional and human qualities make their opinions invaluable to me. Such standing gives them a certain quota of power, which generates enmity inside and outside government circles. Being close to the President and having the inherent influence resulting from being consulted and heard generates jealousy, envy, animosity, verbal attacks from the incompetent, those without the intelligence and ability to compete professionally.

I am a man who has been in many places and positions. In sports, in student movements, in professional, private and public circles. I have many friends and I know many people. I meet with various groups. It's not necessarily a fixed and permanent council, but I turn to different people in different places. That may give the impression at times that I am undecided. It's possible that consulting or pondering may be confused with indecision. I try to be fair and never make a quick decision unless I am absolutely certain it's the right move. For example, when I have to dismiss someone.

I listen carefully and, depending on circumstances, I go with my own analysis and feelings. For instance, if you come with a new idea and it fits into my plans, you will immediately notice a spark in my eyes. I immediately become interested and I say yes and start moving to implement it. Yet for each good idea that interests me there are other 99 I don't go for. So I listen and I say okay, and that'll be the end of it.

Q: *Is there an important decision you have taken without consulting with anybody?*

RDLC: Yes.

Q: *For example?*

RDLC: Many. Small, medium and big. I have a confidential document of strategies and tactics completely written by me, which serves as an agenda to carry out certain tasks, accomplish certain goals, specific priorities. I have sometimes been forced to choose from these personal strategies to make decisions all by myself. Other times I have shared them with one or two people, still others with more people, the cabinet, and even others with the entire people of Guatemala. That's the biggest ring, the popular consultation. In other words, decisions take different procedures, from the ones made in solitude to others made in consultation with one, two, several people and expanded groups. I sometimes consult the cabinet on decisions I've already made but I share them anyway. Other times I consult them before deciding.

Q: *Do you ever consult with your family?*

RDLC: More than consult them, I listen to the important views of my wife and children, though they don't have much influence on my decision-making. From prior positions I've held they are used to not participating much in my decision-making. Including my wife, who has respected me and has restrained herself from becoming too involved. At present, however, my job has a strong resemblance to her own work in the area of social welfare, and we communicate more on work issues.

Sometimes I listen to my children. They share with me

some of the things they hear at the university, which is a good way to get feedback. There have been presidents who have depended totally on their family and wives, to the point that there have been cases in which the spouse has exercised the real power, making important national decisions. I know a couple of presidents who, after making a decision in the cabinet and having it ready for signature and all, would talk to their wives and would back out from their initial decision. This is not my case; I don't have that kind of influence. I listen to them and it's convenient that I do, but that's it. My decisions are not shared, though sometimes my wife and children have shared with me the good and negative feedback they may hear in their circles about actions the government has taken, etc.

I remember a former president who once told me several days of demonstrations against him were taking place in front of the Government Palace, which his closest aides had downplayed telling him that only a handful of people were protesting. It was his wife who finally opened the blinds of the terrace and showed him a huge crowd. The President got very frightened by the fact that, had it not been for his wife, he would have never realized how bad the situation was. We have had presidents in this country who only knew what was going on through comments from their wives.

Q: *How have you managed to gather information about what goes on in the country?*

RDLC: I created an office and coordinated the efforts of various people to feed me information, but I must admit that it's far from perfect. I am a maniac when it comes to being informed. I need a lot of specialized information. For example, in the social care area there has to be a person exclusively devoted to reading all letters, newspapers and obituaries to send condolences. And other more important matters. My secretary constantly evaluates the ministers and analyzes that which would be of interest to me. For instance, say I wish to know the status of a highway under construction, the progress of a specific public work, my secretary follows up on them and informs me. Besides, I receive the army chief of the area who tells me how many kilometers have been completed, etc. So I get a lot of cross-reference information from both civilian and military sources. One way or the other, the President needs to be surrounded by an executive staff. Government is a large enterprise that needs executives who make decisions. The President needs people who are quick executers, so that if we decide to make a statement tomorrow or take certain action in the morning, it cannot get tangled up and forgotten amid the turmoil of my work. I need to forget about the details and have someone carry out the orders. At the same time, the President needs to know all that's going on; he must know reality and not the rosy things he is told.

Q: *Do you use the military often as a more credible source than civilians?*

RDLC: Yes, although I get information from both sides and have permanent analysis teams composed of public and private experts, civilian and military. In general, the military are more disciplined. I have a Presidential Military Staff extraordinarily efficient in every sense of the word, they prepare everything for me. The Military Staff has two main functions: it provides security for the President and his family, and takes care of the logistics of presidential functions. Security includes not only protecting my life, but also my image. They tell me when they hear that something is not functioning well. These are military officers, most of them young, who are carefully trained to work close to the President and his family. They are chosen for their professional qualifications, their merits and discipline, and their performance is extremely efficient. They are very responsible in everything they do and never miss a detail. There are no flaws in a mission they carry out with total commitment in every area — analysis on intelligence, political, social, economic, military and government issues.

Q: *Who controls your schedule?*

RDLC: I control it with the help of the Chief of Protocol, who is a civilian woman. Before it was controlled by the Presidential Military Staff, but I changed this. They control my tours throughout the country. I tease them and tell them that everything is so well organized that I sometimes believe that even people's applause has been prepared and guided. And they act with a lot of discretion and professionalism.

Q: *And with all the violence taking place in the country, if you want to travel, can you move around rapidly or does it take a lot of preparation?*

RDLC: The logical thing is to make arrangements beforehand. This means that I let them know the place I wish to visit and there's an advance team who looks at possible problems. But if I want to get going right away, I do it.

Q: *Can the President go out of the palace alone?*

RDLC: Completely alone, no. The truth is I can't, just as the President of the United States can't go out of the White House alone for security reasons.

Q: *So the military always have to know where the President is going?*

RDLC: That is not really a problem for me. It would be a problem for them if I ever got lost in the streets. I have gone out to the streets without saying where I am headed.

Q: *Do you walk a lot through the streets of Guatemala City?*

RDLC: Of course, although not as much as I would like to. And I visit the soccer stadium frequently. Because of my personality, when I became President I wanted to keep many of my habits. I'm referring to my lifestyle. For example, I wanted to remain living in my own house. To the point that the day of my inauguration there was a reception to honor me in the Government Palace and I didn't go. I called them and said, "Friends, come over to my house and we'll have something to eat here."

I decided to stay in my house because I didn't want to live in the presidential mansion. People liked that. These gestures are well seen by the people. But I couldn't keep away from the presidential mansion for more than three or four days due to various reasons. First of all, there was a security risk going in and out of the house. There was also the fact that I hardly saw my wife and children. So I decided to move in. Besides, it was easier to live in the presidential mansion, which has a tunnel connecting it to the Government Palace, the cabinet conference room, and the rest of the facilities. It was difficult from my private house.

Another decision I made was not to use a whole caravan of vehicles and motorcycles to move around. During the first six months I never used the motorcycle patrol. People don't like to see so many motorcycles sounding their sirens. I later went back to using them for a reason. There was an assassination attempt against me. They found a rifle with a telescopic target in a hotel room in front of a place where I was supposed to be.

Q: *When did this happen?*

RDLC: This happened on June 30, 1994, Army Day. Members of my security staff zeroed in on the suspects and almost captured them, but they managed to escape at the last minute. I think they were people whom I had crushed politically, people who had a lot of power. This incident compelled me to reinforce my security protection. Besides, we've had warnings from intelligence and from embassies who have their own security services. They advise me when they see something unusual. Even so, I have reduced my security guard. It's not large, nothing like it used to be. There have been presidents in this country who had excessive protection, a larger escort than any other president in the world. Totally scandalous and exaggerated.

Another reason for reinstating the motorcycle patrol was that one of the members of the Presidential Military Staff came up to me and said: "Mr. President, it's fine to be discreet, but when we went to the airport today we had to stop 22 times, which is highly dangerous. You could have been the object of an assassination attempt on each of the stops. People applaud your modesty but if we keep doing this someone will stop by our side and leave a bomb, and we will all blow up, including the President's armored vehicle.

I responded that people liked to see us stop at traffic lights, but I understood the risks involved. So we went back to having a motorcycle patrol, whose performance is highly efficient. They use sirens and their own motorcycles to block crossing traffic at intersections so that our cars don't stop at traffic lights. It's more difficult to carry out a terrorist attempt against moving vehicles.

I like to feel free to move, go any place I want to, even walk around. Last year I walked to Congress for a special celebration. And after a dinner with a delegation of Costa Rican union leaders at a hotel, I suggested to walk back. And we did, we walked seven blocks. The president of the University of Costa Rica insisted in taking photographs, arguing that in her country that would have been unusual.

Sometimes I have gone to the stadium to watch a soccer game, and fans have applauded when they have seen me sitting there like any other citizen with my children, enjoying a sports event. I practice soccer and play tennis with my children once or twice a week.

Q: *Don't you agree that the great social revolution in Guatemala would be in place the day the President can walk the streets casually without fearing a military coup or a guerrilla attack?*

RDLC: Absolutely. I imagine that would be the great difference. Also to have an honest president, who would not be insulted for stealing, as has happened some times in the past. Fortunately, that is behind us.

Our country had 10 years of democratic endeavor, from 1944 to 1954, and now we again have a special period. There have been very few moments of reform in Guatemala, much less of peaceful change, without bloodshed. What we need here is a true cultural revolution, not in the Chinese style. A cultural and moral revolution that ended the culture of violence and allowed mutual understanding and honesty. We should learn to reward dialogue and remove from our lives the obsession of imposition and the blunt kick.

What I would like in the political area is to preserve the institutions, to end the confrontation between civilians and the military. And, above all, to never again have to deal with purges and dishonest people. I had to clean up the legislative and judicial branches of government. There is a new Congress and a new Supreme Court that are not involved in scandals. I don't wish any other president that experience. A purge is a terrible thing and we were fortunate to have done it without spilling a drop of blood. Yet I agree that the great revolution in this country must be cultural, educational, moral, without weapons and bloodshed.

In human rights terms, 1995 should be called the year of peace. Not only for ending the internal armed confrontation, but for beginning the social and economic peace which the government is pursuing through its political will. We need to culminate our negotiations with the URNG in a move toward absolute respect for the individual rights of Guatemalans and the strengthening of the judicial system to prevent impunity. That's another great fight with which to end our term this year. To totally erase impunity from our system. Also to continue our fight against poverty by means of an honest, transparent investment in health, education and the necessary infrastructure.

Another goal has to do with security for our citizens. I am aware of the serious problems people are facing. The government will give priority to drastic short- and medium-term measures to fight crime and violence fostered by a few bad Guatemalans who threaten the peaceful life of families of various status in our society.

In 1995 we have maintained our institutional reinforcement by means of restoring the credibility of all government institutions. The changes in Congress and the Supreme Court were crucial for this, and we will continue the fight against corruption so that the honest and effective exercise of government functions can consolidate our law-abiding democratic system. I have just replaced the Interior Minister, something unprecedented in the history of Guatemala. Never before had a minister been dismissed to be investigated and eventually tried for an alleged act of corruption that wasn't yet proven. Especially with an Interior Minister. This has been exemplary and the people have received it well. It doesn't matter if it placed me in a difficult position because he was a dear friend whom I wanted to keep in the government ranks. But I had to make that decision for state reasons.

Finally, in 1995 we will have elections, and they will be peaceful and transparent. Because there's no official party, no government resources nor mechanisms will be available for any party or candidate. This new electoral process will undoubtedly energize our democracy as a way of life.

Guatemala and the CIA

By Santiago Aroca

Relations between Guatemala and the United States suffered a serious setback when it was discovered in the spring of 1995 that Guatemalan officers on the payroll of the U.S. Central Intelligence Agency were involved in kidnaping, rapes and killings in the Central American country.

The accusations made public in the United States left the espionage agency in disarray and without much support in Washington ranks.

U.S. Rep. Robert Torricelli, a Democrat from New Jersey, denounced in April of 1995 that people receiving money from the CIA killed U.S. citizens in Guatemala. Torricelli wrote President Bill Clinton that CIA collaborators continued receiving a salary from the agency years after committing the crimes.

Torricelli's letter to the President coincided with a sensitive moment for the CIA since the future of the intelligence community in the United States had come under investigation by the White House. One of the issues under discussion was a drastic reduction of CIA's budget and its agents. Further, the CIA was without leadership since the resignation of director R. James Woolsey in December of 1994. The person temporarily in charge of the agency, Adm. William O. Studeman, told Congress he had no time to clarify the events in Guatemala and that it had to wait for the Administration to appoint a new CIA director.

The agency does not hide it has been helping Guatemala since in 1954 a coup toppled the pro-Communist government of Jacobo Arbenz. However, no U.S. president before Clinton had ever been placed in the position of having to explain why thousands of taxpayers' dollars ended in the pockets of people who killed U.S. citizens.

At the core of the controversy there are two killings. The first one took place in June of 1990, when a group of Guatemalan soldiers killed an American innkeeper named Michael DeVine for reasons still unclear. He was taken by people in uniform from his inn at Poptun, in the middle of the jungle, and was later found dead. The Guatemalan judicial system opened an investigation that ended with the incarceration of five soldiers and an officer. The soldiers are serving a 30-year sentence, but the officer escaped from prison. Guatemalan authorities have asked Interpol for help to capture him.

The second killing was of guerrilla leader Efraín Bámaca. His death took place in 1992 and was not confirmed by U.S. officials until April of 1995, when Torricelli broke the news to Bámaca's widow, American attorney Jennifer Harbury. According to Torricelli, the killing was supervised by a high-ranking Guatemalan officer, Col. Julio Roberto Alpírez, a graduate from the Fort Benning School of the Americas in Georgia, where approximately 60,000 Latin American officers have been trained in the last few decades.

Tension between the two countries

was aggravated when after the Torricelli statement various U.S. officials quoted the CIA as saying the Guatemalan military was plotting Harbury's assassination.

The White House said it couldn't confirm the information, but FBI agents traveled to Austin, Texas, to protect Harbury. A State Department spokesperson added it had contacted the Guatemalan authorities requesting pertinent action to find the authors of the conspiracy.

Harbury said that on April 12 FBI agents told her Guatemalan government officials were recruiting professional hit-men to assassinate her while she was in one of her hunger strikes. She added the agents never revealed their informant's identity nor told her whether they had verified the information through independent means. Harbury fears that, if true, the Guatemalans may have been trying to kill her since she started her hunger strikes in front of the Guatemalan embassy in Washington in the fall of 1994.

Amid the tension generated by these events, a Boston court fined former Guatemalan Defense Minister Gen. Héctor Gramajo with $47.5 million for the detention and torture of 11 Guatemalans and an American nun. Gramajo argued that the court ruling was as absurd as imposing a fine of $47.5 million on former U.S. Defense Secretary Robert McNamara for the atrocities committed by American soldiers in My Lai during the Vietnam war.

At first, Guatemalans reacted to the controversy nervously. President Ramiro de León Carpio said initially that there was no evidence to support the accusations against Col. Alpírez. In fact, he advised Col. Alpírez to sue Torricelli for slander. A few days later, however, after the weight of the evidence began to mount, President De León Carpio instructed the nation's General Prosecutor to open an investigation and ordered Col. Alpírez dismissed from the army.

Efraín Bámaca's death was especially calamitous for the CIA. What separated this death from that of other 110,000 people in Guatemala since 1978 was the fact that Col. Alpírez was a CIA agent and the agency knew of his involvement in the death of Michael DeVine. Try as they might to find a scapegoat, Torricelli's denunciation revealed the huge structural flaws inside the CIA.

The scandal also played a part in the power struggle of some segments of the Democratic Party with President Clinton to control foreign policy. Torricelli is the author of the Cuba Democracy Act passed in 1992 tightening the U.S. trade embargo against Cuba. Important White House security advisers, among them Anthony Lake, head of the National Security Council, have shown an inclination to lift the embargo at least partially. With his denunciation Torricelli may have tried to embarrass Lake before the CIA.

To Guatemalans, this is not an interesting debate. In Guatemala the scandal had two implications. First, it showed to what extent the Guatemalan military was penetrated by the CIA. To a significant number of Guatemalan officers, Alpírez is a traitor, an agent of a foreign superpower that in 1978, under Jimmy Carter's administration, had deprived their country of technical assistance in protest for abuses committed by the Guatemalan military. The second implication is the political dichotomy whereby the military must respond for its human rights violations, not so the guerrillas.

In the United States the debate was totally different. The media jumped with the usual skepticism at statements coming from high-ranking White House and State Department officials saying they did not know about CIA activities. In general, CIA carries out its work in Latin America under a don't-ask-don't tell policy. The Administration never asks the agency what it's doing and the agency looks the other way from what goes on among its collaborators.

In the Bámaca case, top U.S. officials have denied having any knowledge. U.S. Secretary of State Warren Christopher appeared on television in April of 1995 alleging he did not know payments were still being made to Guatemalan officers. He pledged they would stop immediately. Political analysts received these words with skepticism. One wrote that, after 30 years of waging a Cold War that no longer exists, the agency was like a transatlantic liner drifting erratically.

The CIA problems in Guatemala may date as far back as the 50s, when the postwar status was altered and the United States and the Soviet Union embarked in confrontations in multiple scenarios. Korea, Vietnam and Latin America became disputed territory. The Soviets failed in Guatemala, but years later Fidel Castro won in Cuba. For years, American taxpayers footed expensive bills for an enormous intelligence effort that frequently went beyond the democratic society the United States were supposed to be defending.

In Argentina and Chile, for example, the CIA collaborated with security forces that later committed serious abuse and left a death trail of thousands. No one has asked publicly in Washington what were the CIA's responsibilities in counterinsurgence activities that claimed the lives of many in the continent.

This is why the Bámaca case was so devastating to the CIA. The death of DeVine marked a moment of tension in the relations between both countries. Then-U.S. Ambassador Thomas F. Stroock vigorously protested and requested an investigation. Stroock was convinced the military were responsible for DeVine's death and Alpírez was at the core of the crime. What the ambassador didn't know was that Alpírez received an envelope from his embassy every month.

Even so, in 1990 the U.S. embassy in Guatemala asked permission from the Justice Department in Washington to interrupt all relations with Alpírez and initiate a process that would lead to his indictment in the United States for the death of the American innkeeper. It took the Justice Department six months to respond that, after studying the case, DeVine's death was not an act of terrorism and therefore no action could be taken in the United States against Alpírez. There was thus no impediment for Alpírez to receive a final payment from the CIA of $44,000 in July of 1992, just after Bámaca's disappearance.

It's hard to tell how high a price the CIA will have to pay for so many errors. In June, the White House published a report clearing the agency and placing total responsibility in Alpírez's hands. However, the final verdict rests with the group of 17 experts commissioned to render a report in 1996 to determine whether the CIA should continue to exist and what its area of activity should be.

The ultimate irony is how the death of two persons in a small country like Guatemala could derail the most feared institution in the United States — the victorious Cold War contestant CIA.

15

Uncle Sam, Castro's Cuba and Belize

Question: *How difficult are the relations between Guatemala and the United States?*

Ramiro de León Carpio: Good. This doesn't mean there are no problems. We want more concessions in the area of trade, more possibilities of exporting to the United States, and sometimes we find that great country to be somewhat protectionist. I am among those who believe there is too much aid and not enough free trade. This should not be interpreted as a desire to give up cooperation from the United States or from any other developed country. Yet it is important that we are allowed to sell in their markets. They are rich and our big opportunity is there, but on the basis of legitimate free market and open competition on equal standing.

Ever since I became President relations with the United States have been highly satisfactory. I believe they appreciate our human rights efforts.

Q: *From a historical perspective, in Guatemala, as in other Central*

American countries, relations with the United States have been tense. Are there many scars left?

RDLC: Scars in certain periods have been deeper than in others, but history itself is now offering a different perspective. In the case of Guatemala current relations are excellent. At some point, the United States decided to help the cause of democracy and encouraged the establishment of democratic regimes. Unfortunately, in the past they helped and supported dictatorships. We are part of the wave of democratization in Latin America. Before, you had to talk to the empire. Things have changed and, in the case of Guatemala, relations are excellent, although we still have problems in the area of human rights. We are still under threatening conditions, like not giving us access to a certain market or imposing a new norm, but again this is part of the complicated nature of relations between neighbors. Particularly when the neighbor is big and you are so small.

Q: *Does the United States currently grant any economic aid to Guatemala?*

RDLC: Yes, significant aid in every sense for certain areas. Yet we must separate the areas; that is, one thing is the economic area and another is the commercial and political areas. Especially now that we have a democratic system and an honest government we shouldn't be threatened with certain penalties for the inheritances of the past. For example, for a problem with an American brutally murdered sometime back. It's a horrible crime, no doubt about it, but the present Guatemalan administration has nothing to do with it nor do the people. One person has been convicted and is in prison. The process is still open for other suspects.

Q: *Is it positive that the President of the United States is concerned about human rights in Guatemala?*

RDLC: Indeed. Human rights violations must be denounced wherever they take place. It doesn't matter what country it is nor can it be argued that it is a sovereignty issue. The only thing I resent is that the United States didn't worry about human rights in Guatemala before, when they supported military dictatorships.

When I was Human Rights Commissioner I received cooperation from the international community and I had total support from the United States. The problem is that the United States has an erratic policy toward Latin America.

The issue here is that they don't go back to the past, when they used to appoint and remove presidents. There were times they backed ruthless dictatorships and gave money to corrupt administrations, which led to indebtedness. Opinion polls in Latin America often show a generalized resentment at the United States.

In general, I do believe that we Central Americans admire the United States, especially its people. We like them and admire their respect for democracy. We have no vocation for servility although we do have respect for a nation's greatness. We respect the empire, but we approach it with dignity, certainly not kneeling. This is how people feel. We must accept and request American help, and we are grateful to receive, again with national dignity. This is what's happened during the last decade, when things have actually changed. The common interest in democracy and human rights brings our two nations closer together and makes collaboration more efficient.

Q: *One of the latest crisis in relations between Guatemala and the United States was prompted by accusations that children were being kidnaped to deliver them to American families. How badly were these relations affected?*

RDLC: Relations did not suffer at the government level. As I said before, we have excellent relations. The things I have just said I've said clearly, openly and frankly. Unfortunately, there were two or three cases that attracted a lot of publicity against Guatemala. Children stolen and transported abroad, children's organs exported. This was the work of meanspirited people who don't love Guatemala. It generated a tremendous psychosis that led to xenophobia against Americans who people thought came to take our children away. A manipulated publicity campaign for which our tourism sector had to pay a high price. I must add that we had very fruitful meetings with U.S. envoys who helped us solve the problem.

Q: *Does that mean hostility against foreigners has ceased among the population?*

RDLC: Right. The action taken eliminated the problem.

Q: *Was there a political intention behind all of this?*

RDLC: I don't have the slightest doubt there was.

Q: *How many cases were there, two?*

RDLC: Only two cases that were extremely publicized, manipulated, orchestrated with the sole purpose of harming Guatemala.

Q: *Relations with Cuba has been another important factor in Guatemala's foreign policy. You have promoted encounters in favor of Cuba's democratization. Why?*

RDLC: Because we will support whatever helps Cubans reach agreement to improve their situation. It will help the rest of their neighbors.

Q: *Are you in favor or against lifting the U.S. embargo against Cuba?*

RDLC: That's part of the negotiations. In other words, democratization and the embargo will have to be resolved in the same agreement, within the same dialogue. The ideal would be to negotiate and compromise on specific goals. If those goals really begin to materialize toward a democratic system in Cuba, I believe things will have to begin changing and eventually Cuba's participation in hemispheric forums could strengthen the inter-American system.

Q: *Do you believe the Cuban government is capable of agreeing to terms in a negotiation, of meeting deadlines and making concessions? What makes you think Fidel Castro would do this?*

RDLC: That's a good question; better yet, a big question mark. If Fidel Castro has really considered that he can't live under that blockade and feels he must participate openly with the rest of the countries, both politically and economically; and if he is conscious of the harm inflicted on his people by the blockade, the hope is that he may be convinced to open up and give in.

On the other hand, when we Latin American presidents have met with him in annual summits, especially in the 1994 summit in Cartagena de Indias, Colombia, we have spoken to him very frankly. We have expressed to him our love for the Cuban people and have sincerely offered to meet as often as he wants. Unfortunately, his response has always been totally negative, although it may be because of the moral pressure. That's why I say it's a big question mark. If he were to be convinced that at some point change is inevitable, why not do it peacefully and avoid a bigger disaster and bloodshed? But I'm not sure whether he is convinced of that reality.

Q: *When you meet Fidel Castro to discuss the Cuban situation, can you forget the contribution Cuba has made to Central Americans conflicts?*

RDLC: No. It is hard. In those moments I try to be a statesman and act coldly. It is logical that for us Central Americans — especially El Salvador, Nicaragua, and more specifically Guatemala — it is hard to put aside the fact that many of the weapons, resources and training of the Guatemalan guerrillas came from Cuba and Fidel Castro, and that many of our dead, widows and orphans are the result of Fidel Castro's decision. It's so hard because he has been the enemy of Guatemala; not only of our governments, but of the Guatemalan people who have been seriously hurt — especially the poorest, the peasants from the indigenous communities who suffered most of the deaths.

It's hard, but, as I have said, I assume the attitude of a statesman who tries to see it all from the humanitarian standpoint. My ever-prevailing principle that perhaps one life could be saved makes talking to him worthwhile.

Q: *You offered a meeting in Guatemala, specifically in Esquipulas, for all Cubans to meet and find a solution to the problems of the island. How did the United States react to this?*

RDLC: Knowing the way they act and the State Department's usual reaction, they must have had some reservations and doubts about where this project was headed. Not in Guatemala, though. We have clarity on this. We want peace for our brothers on the island. And I believe that the Americans, as the project gains clarity, will end up collaborating with it. They can't oppose it; they shouldn't, since the process follows a line of peaceful democratization. However, Fidel's opinion and response are needed if this well-intentioned project is to work at all.

Q: *The Cuban community in the United States always reproaches Latin America for being too soft on Fidel Castro. What is your opinion about this?*

RDLC: I have often heard presidents in different Latin American countries talk about Cuba as a victim, a country living under the American blockade. What they fail to see is that Cuba lives under its own internal blockade.

Some people feel the proposed forum in Guatemala interferes with Cuba's internal affairs. But can anybody think of bigger interference than to train, arm and equip illegal groups to invade Guatemala and spread terror and death among children, youths, elderly, and harm the nation's infrastructure? That was real interference. Our sovereignty and interests were shattered. I feel I have a right to address the issue of Cuba and, more and more, people are getting a better sense of the real problem, to the point that almost all nations in the hemisphere are beginning to realize that they have been soft, and in every meeting more voices are raised to ask Fidel Castro to make changes.

Q: *Why do you participate so often in these meetings with your colleagues, the Central American presidents, to discuss Cuba?*

RDLC: Why I do it? The answer is simple — the fact that I am President doesn't make me forget my vocation and values. I consider it my duty to protect human rights. And when someone who has championed and continues to champion the cause of human rights knows of a violation — be it here in Guatemala, China, Peru, Cuba, or wherever — he can't but feel outraged, hurt and motivated to take action within his possibilities.

Human rights are violated in Cuba. Freedom, the most sacred individual right, is suppressed. Someone argued that economic rights are respected because health and education worked well. It's true and we must acknowledge it. Perfect. Fine. But the right to freedom, from which all other rights originate, is not respected.

As far as I am concerned, I am a former Human Rights Commissioner and I will continue to defend the human rights of any person, whether in prison or out of prison, military or civilian, poor or rich, of whatever race and religion, here or in any other part of the world. That is a mission no one can keep me from carrying out. Only when God takes my life will I stop protecting and promoting human rights. It's an inherent mission in me.

You might ask, if the President of Guatemala has not resolved the problem of human rights in his own country, how can he resolve the problem of others? It's very clear that we have problems here and we must fix them. But if I can contribute to improve respect for human rights in other countries, I will do so.

I always say that my greatest satisfaction has been to have saved the life of one or various persons. If I have felt satisfied for saving a life in Guatemala, how can I not be pleased to contribute to save the life of a nation and its freedom? And this does not mean in any way that my government and I are interfering with other people's self-determination. My intention is to find a way to help the Cuban people resolve the problems they have.

As President, I and my Central American colleagues, have had the opportunity to talk with representatives of the Cuban opposition in exile and inside Cuba. We talked about the possibility of contributing our painful experience with armed internal confrontations, absence of democracy, human rights violations, and the solutions we found. We always used dialogue and peaceful negotiations, rationalizing on the many problems we had. And if that approach worked here, why can't it work in Cuba? That's where the idea of the forum came from. A forum to analyze the inter-American system, since all the presidents and the entire continent are concerned that Cuba does not participate in the Inter-American Integration System.

For Cuba to join us it will have to comply with certain requisites, among them to be a democratic nation like the rest of us. Unfortunately, that is not the case, and that's what's keeping it from entering the organization.

With the purpose of uniting Cuba, integrating it to the rest of the continent, we have proposed a forum to discuss Cuba's crucial issues with all Cubans.

Q: *Including the opposition?*

RDLC: Yes, inside and outside Cuba. And all sectors — political, religious, labor, etc. — and, of course, the government. In other words, to invite them all to probably the first forum ever, but one to be followed by others, where the Cuban situation can be analyzed in all its depth.

Q: *Do you have any realistic hopes that the government of Fidel Castro will accept an invitation to participate in a forum of this nature?*

RDLC: We have talked to Fidel Castro, and we decided to wait because without his acquiescence the project would not be viable. But we will continue talking to him.

I believe that if we work hard on this, he will realize it is a serious effort and not an ambush to seek advantage, that its sole purpose is to dialogue about Cuba and find peace. I have hopes that the entire Cuban society will be represented there.

Q: *Allow me to change scenarios. As opposed to most of the Central American nations that drag historical feuds with all their neighbors, Guatemala has problems only with Belize. In the past it has even been the cause of military tension. What is the current status of Belize in Guatemala?*

RDLC: In the Constitutional Assembly we resolved the Belize issue, which up to then had been one of our biggest controversies, with our transitional Article 19. For years the Constitution included Belize as part of Guatemala and everyone here seemed to agree with the phrase "Belize is ours." The truth is that, internationally, Belize does not belong to Guatemala. Its independence is recognized by the international community and the issue boiled down to a territorial dispute, which was a lot easier to resolve.

Q: *Did President Cerezo negotiate the Belize issue to find a Constitutional solution?*

RDLC: Yes, he participated in the negotiations based on the transitional clauses established in Article 19 of our Constitution. This article empowers the Executive branch to seek a solution to the rights of Guatemala regarding Belize in conformity with national interests. It also specifies that any definitive accord must be submitted to Congress and to the procedure of public referendum established by Article 173 of the Constitution, which also allows the government of Guatemala to promote social, economic and cultural relations with the people of Belize.

Translated into practice, this means that now we can talk, negotiate and coexist with Belize. This was virtually impossible before under the false argument that, without a question, Belize belonged to Guatemala. The current flexibility allows us to continue negotiating. Belize is now recognized as a free state by the United Nations.

My administration has put together a group of ideally qualified people to serve on an Accessory Board on Belize to make preparations toward a new negotiation. If agreement is reached and we sign an accord at government level, we could then take it to a referendum which, if approved, could conclude the case of Belize.

Q: *Guatemala has a long history of integrating Central America. Guatemala housed the General Headquarters and the Central American Federation. What is the current status of integration?*

RDLC: Fairly good because in Central America we managed to overcome our possible differences. For years we dreamed of a common Central American state, but integration had failed due to our tremendous political instability. Today we have democracy and sufficient stability for a fresh attempt.

Q: *Any new attempts to form a Central American common market? In the sixties one of these attempts failed, did it not?*
RDLC: It failed because of extreme instability then. Besides, internal economic interests could not reach agreement. No way could be found for the great economic interests in Central America to agree on a modus operandi. But the most serious cause was political instability. It was a pity. When I worked in the Economic Integration Department in the 60s we could have made progress, but in 1967 and 1968 the war between El Salvador and Honduras, compounded by the political instability, shattered any possibility of integrating or creating a common market.

Now the situation is different. All Central American countries are governed by a democratic system and all internal armed clashes and wars have ceased, except in Guatemala, whose own confrontation is close to an end. Our present governments have shown a clear determination to integrate, not only because conditions have changed, but because of the personality and interrelation of the presidents. Even Costa Rica, which had been the most reluctant to integration, today champions Central American efforts. We signed the protocol for the Economic Integration Treaty in the IV Central American Summit held in Guatemala at the end of 1993.

We now account for unprecedented decisions and attitudes in political, economic and social areas. I am convinced that all Central American countries must act in bloc, as we have done with the United States, Mexico, Colombia, Venezuela. Never before has Central America reached a moment as favorable to integration and with more political determination to act accordingly.

16

A Legacy of Democratic Achievements

Question: *Regarding NAFTA, the North American Free Trade Agreement integrating the economies of Canada, the United States and Mexico, the Central American bloc has wanted a negotiation with that group. Would any of you negotiate separately or would you always do it as a bloc?*

Ramiro de León Carpio: We have expressed our desire to negotiate as a bloc, though Costa Rica, for example, has bilateral agreements with Mexico. After signing the Central American Integration Treaty we agreed not to negotiate nor sign accords bilaterally. Although not all countries liked this arrangement, we have continued talking and have agreement on banana and coffee, as well as on a sustained development vis-a-vis the United States and the world.

Q: *Do you believe that entering NAFTA is anywhere close?*

RDLC: Well, there's a mechanism that allows entrance in two years. We have applied and are preparing ourselves for the earliest possible date. All three countries in NAFTA are receptive and we believe that, yes, the possibility may be near. We need to work hard and be totally ready in two years.

Q: *Is the Central American Parliament, which has its headquarters in Guatemala, following that integration process? What is your view on the parliament?*

RDLC: In my opinion, the real Central American Parliament is yet to be established. What we have now is an interesting forum without a driving engine toward integration. It lacks protagonism and needs to persuade Central American people of its reason to exist. In the latest Central American summit held in Costa Rica I insisted that the moment was ripe for our decision and we needed to decide whether we wanted a parliament. The consensus was affirmative. So we began a process oriented to have our respective populations recognize and accept the parliament as something useful. The problem has been that the concept of parliament is viewed as something useless, though it could perform activities and functions terribly important to Central America.

In our integration efforts, for example, it could occupy a predominant place vis-a-vis the European Parliament, the European Union and the international community as a whole. It would be a respectable front, probably with more impact abroad that in our countries, but with important social tasks to carry out within our populations. The reason for the criticism on this side is mainly the salaries of its members, who are perceived as people who have no functions and do nothing.

Q: *Doesn't too much concentration on Central America make you lose sight of other parts of the world?*

RDLC: Not really. What happens is that we have intense relations with our neighbors — Costa Rica, Honduras, El Salvador, Nicaragua and Panama. But we don't forget about the rest. For instance, we recently completed an agreement with Mexico on Central American sugar, of which Guatemala will export 50 percent given its larger capacity. The other half of the contract was spread among the rest of the Central American countries.

Q: *Will there ever be a president of Central America?*
RDLC: It would be difficult. It's a yearning that in some manner took wings with the Latin American Parliament — the dream of Simón Bolívar, José Martí, and many others — but at the Central American level. I believe some day we will have the great Central American fatherland Francisco Morazán dreamed about. It would be a wonderful and useful concept, but I see it as a difficult, far away utopia. Indeed, a beautiful ideal to talk about in forums and political speeches about Central American unity, but extraordinarily remote.
Q: *After your experience as President, is it worthwhile to devote one's life to politics, or is it highly risky in a country like Guatemala?*
RDLC: I do not tolerate violence, I can't stand injustice, and I love freedom. Around these three topics the 53 years of my life have transpired. The humanitarian sense and social sensitivity have always been present, and ethical and religious values have governed my life. Honesty has been my best banner in all my acts as a private and public man and as a politician and president.

The presidency is a difficult challenge. I feel satisfaction in spite of the sacrifices it has imposed on my family life. My family was not accustomed to this type of experience. As a politician I assimilate the blows, the criticism, even affront. Not my wife; she has had to endure the fact that the First Family is the most visible and criticized, the one getting most of the verbal attacks and insults. She was not used to politics, but I am proud of how well she has performed.

In spite of all, it was worth it because the general interests prevail over our own, and what we are doing pleases me tremendously. I believe I will end my term with the satisfaction of accomplishing what was needed, albeit within my means. Already it has greatly gratified me to go out and make direct contact with the people, to stand receptive to the requests from people — children, youngsters, the elderly — who come to tell me they're praying for me. They understand my position is very difficult and they wish me well: "God bless you, Mr. President," they tell me. It's been a rough road but not leading to a dead end. The goal is near and I must reach it with the joy that I made the right sacrifices and gave this challenge my best effort. Like the chess player who reaches the endgame with the confidence that he is winning.

In only a few months my constitutional term will end and, through my great strategies and countless tactics, I have been able to accomplish that which I set for myself.

Q: *Final question: Which goals did you accomplish and which are still pending?*

RDLC: The goals accomplished can be summarized as follows: 1) In the institutional/military area I was able to rescue, preserve and strengthen the nation's institutionality. Today no one in Guatemala imagines the possibility of a constitutional breach; the *coups d'etat* remain as part of our sad history. They are in the past and our democracy is strong. 2) In the political field, I accomplished what the people asked and demanded of me, such as the purge of government bodies. I achieved a new Congress and a new Supreme Court. As a result, the General Prosecution Office was created under an independent Public Ministry, as well as a totally autonomous General Comptroller. But most importantly, all this renovation was executed by taking the most difficult of roads — the legal path of popular consultation, of democracy, without spilling a drop of blood. I achieved political stability. Furthermore, the constitutional reforms, all directed to perfect the democratic system and its functions via the independence of its institutions, and designed to fight political corruption. For the first time ever in the history of Guatemala our Constitution was reformed without upsetting our institutional order. 3) In the economic area, from the macroeconomic standpoint, stability was attained in currency exchange and in monetary and credit policies. Inflation was kept within a range from 8 to 11 percent, and our monetary reserves rose considerably. External debt, one of the lowest in Latin America, was kept in check, while economic growth reached 4.5 percent of the Gross Internal Product on its route to the 1995 goal of 5 percent, an attainable figure given the growth of exports, especially of non-traditional goods, and the increase of tourism. There is confidence in national and foreign investment despite the security and violence problems in Guatemala, which are no different than in most countries in the world. A Tax Reform package was established, giving the government an additional revenue of some 1,670 million quetzals (approximately $417.5 million), a 30 percent increment, to be applied to the fight against poverty and meeting other social needs. From the legal and administrative point of view, this represents a clean-up in our public finances that will result in more resources for the next government to achieve improved levels of investment and social spending. The decline in tax revenue I found when I took office was halted and reversed, leading to increased collection levels. In part because of tax reform and government efforts in the area of public spending and improving revenue, the International Monetary Fund approved the Shadow Accord with Guatemala, setting a 1.3 percent goal for global deficit, represented by a quasi-fiscal deficit of 1 percent from operational losses of the Bank of Guatemala; a 0.8 percent fiscal deficit; and a 5 percent surplus from the rest of public entities. All in relation to the Gross Internal Product. Our net international monetary reserves amount to US$800 million, which is equivalent to three months of imports and a range of inflation levels established by the government. The positive angle of this accord is that it gives Guatemala credibility before the international financial community, granting support to my economic policy and attracting foreign capital for investment in our country. 4) In the social domain, my government's agenda also defined a clear strategy that, in spite of financial difficulties, has led to the improvements I now summarize. For the first time in many years the budget execution in investment expenses reached 76 percent of what was planned. It is expected that in 1995 this investment level will be surpassed. It's important to highlight the priority my government gave to social investment, with budgeted appropriations at unprecedented levels in the areas of health and education. Additional mechanisms (social funds) were created, such as the Solidarity Fund through the development councils, and the allocation to FONAPAZ (National Fund for Peace) increased more than 100 percent. The FIS (Social Investment Fund) was also given high priority. The Indigenous Development Fund and the Housing Fund were created, granting constitutional contributions to municipalities for local investment. All these measures work toward the goal of genuinely fighting poverty while setting irreversible bases for continuation by future governments. Another important aspect is that as part of my strategy to fight poverty I gave high priority to starting a culture of social participation never before experienced in our history. This principle has sparked various society activators to unite the efforts of the central and local governments with those of the people toward community development. This tripartite action has strengthened administrative decentralization and could lead to an authentic revolution of opinion and participation by all segments of society. This is already being done with confidence, especially among peasants and indigenous communities in rural areas. I also showed my political determination by moving toward administrative decentralization, giving more power to local authorities and encouraging them to make decisions that before could only be made in the government palace. This allows them to identify and prioritize their needs, such as the selection and appointment of teachers, the installation of offices of the Finance Ministry in the country's regional departments, the distribution of resources directly to the favored communities and to the Regional Development Councils. By moving toward administrative, economic and fiscal decentralization I was able to show the people of Guatemala that a government can act with honesty, transparence and austerity, transferring resources based on the real priorities of the people. This behavior establishes a precedent which must be observed by future governments.

In this same area I reached the goal of eliminating the presidency's millionaire confidential funds, which in the past served as a source of corruption. Through the Constitutional Reform these funds were later eliminated throughout all departments of government to guarantee that in the future no corruption can result from such funds. With regard to the peace efforts, all four areas of government — military, political, economic and social — have made significant progress through accords already subscribed which, independently from the final agreement, move the nation closer to the structural transformation it needs.

There are three interrelated areas that need reinforcement: respect for human rights, peace, and the elimination of any form of impunity. The moment I took office I set for myself the central goal of attaining a firm and durable peace for Guatemala, and I have gone all out in my efforts to achieve it. Toward such objective I have instituted respect for individual human rights — the right to life, physical integrity, freedom, security — and I have moved toward eliminating our greatest evil: war. Furthermore, I have worked hard in favor of economic and social development to improve the life style of our citizens, their health, education, jobs, housing, nutrition and environment. Guatemala must continue its struggle to eliminate impunity and I have taken and will continue to take steps in that direction throughout the rest of my period, such as investigation, trial and punishment for those responsible of human rights violations, common crimes, and other unlawful conduct. Among these measures will be the dissolution of the Military Commissioners and other actions related to Civil Defense Patrols.

Another area requiring a major effort is citizen security. Although I never expected to resolve a problem of which the causes are structural, I intended to improve the personal safety of all Guatemalans with timely measures — emergency, short- and long-term action — to establish the foundation that will allow the future government to advance in this area.

Resources were transferred to improve the compensation of the police force by means of a risk bonus, as well as to equip them better for their fight against crime. I also have coordinated all efforts within internal forces in their war against drug-trafficking and organized crime. Having said this, there still are structural reasons, political and economic, that have lately been responsible for increasing the level of insecurity, despite the efforts that had been effective initially in our problems of citizen security. Financial priority has been given to law-enforcement institutions, duly reinforced by the creation of the General Prosecution Office under the Public Ministry, as well as the Supreme Court, whose budgets will be increased by 2 percent.

Finally, the entire national media acknowledge that my government has totally respected freedom of speech and freedom of the press. And those who know our sad and dismal history realize that the goals accomplished and the progress achieved in our country, small as they may be and given the harsh circumstances, are greatly appreciated and represent a step forward in the reinforcement of a democratic system that, for the first time in our country, bears substantiated hopes of lasting as the best way of life for our people.

Epilogue

The last time I visited him, sitting in his presidential office and talking over coffee, I asked Ramiro de León Carpio what were his expectations of the future. His response startled me.

"To hand over the presidency and watch my successor enjoy it with reasonable prudence, to the applause of my compatriots."

I found this extremely unusual. Politicians hardly ever wish their successors well, and it is infrequent to devote any thoughts to their performance.

Guatemala is now different. President De León Carpio will pass on the presidency to a person elected by his peers. It may sound simple and obvious to the fortunate inhabitants of three dozen countries, but it amounts to a dream to millions of human beings condemned to live in a cycle of misery, repression, hardship.

I do not know how history will judge the decisions made by Ramiro de León Carpio's administration, but of one thing

I am certain: he will have achieved what many thought was impossible — to transfer power to a successor elected in free elections. It has not occurred often in the history of Guatemala. To be more precise: it will be the second time it happens within the institutions of the Central American country. And the fact that the person transferring power is a human rights activist to whom no abuses can be attributed makes it all much more meaningful.

When he took office, many thought President De León Carpio would not be capable of controlling the military or that his personality was too weak to handle the upheavals of power.

The core decisions of his government have combined the pursuits of economic progress with the consolidation of democratic institutions. On both counts he will leave the presidency with a solid record.

In the area of the armed forces, there have been significant transformations. First and foremost, the military no longer controls civilian power. All the contrary, advance on the road to democratic consolidation has reached a point where the country's armed forces face two problems now encouragingly common to other Latin American nations: the reduction of their size and the screening of responsibilities for past abuses. In both areas, vital for their survival, the armed forces have had to accept decisions from the civilian power.

On June 30, 1995, President De León Carpio abolished by decree the concept of Military Commissioners, sinister liaisons between the armed forces and civilians who for decades had abused their powers. Further, early in his presidential term he eliminated the Intelligence Unit, popularly known as "The Archive" and repeatedly accused of abuse.

Guatemala has not been an exception in the trend of democratic normalization. Yet it travels a peculiar road as the only Central American nation still suffering a guerrilla war.

In Guatemala there is still fighting between its regular army and rebel forces. Not with the intensity of the past, but still at the expense of innocent lives while both sides make attempts to sit at the negotiating table.

Under crossfire, subjected to the pressures of a society submerged in bloodshed, President De León Carpio has kept his ground — no human rights violations will be allowed, and whoever commits them will end up in court. This rule is as valid to the guerrillas as to the government's security forces. It would be fair to say that Guatemala is a society still with too much violence, but where impunity is reaching a dead end.

The most clear example is the President's behavior in what many consider the thorniest problems he has had to face — the cases known as the "Bámaca and the DeVine affairs."

From the beginning, President De León Carpio said no one responsible for crimes or wrongdoing would be protected. The results are on the table. There is close collaboration with the U.S. State Department and the U.S. embassy in Guatemala to exchange information that could clarify the circumstances and the culprits of the death of guerrilla commander Efraín Bámaca. The same procedure has been followed in the death of U.S. citizen Michael DeVine. By orders from President De León Carpio, all members of the armed forces involved in these cases, as in other serious human rights violations, have been separated from their offices. Further, the military information services have been substantially restructured.

In other words, from the presidency, De León Carpio has kept the same pugnacious behavior as he had when he has Human Rights Commissioner.

Of course, there's a lot to be done yet. De León Carpio's successor inherits the military problem, albeit within parameters that allow solutions. Particularly if, as expected, there is significant progress in the peace negotiations with the guerrillas and they give up their armed struggle.

On economic progress, the character traits of Ramiro de León Carpio have made a positive impact. In a country accustomed to rulers who imposed their will with the use of weapons if necessary, De León Carpio has used an altogether different approach to power: consensus. His presidency has stayed course, despite harassment and crises, thanks to his extraordinary ability to form alliances in resolving grave problems.

A good example of his effective style was seen when a part of the business sector boycotted his tax reform and, overnight, the country was placed on the verge of bankruptcy by a court sentence annulling the tax system introduced by the government.

It was indeed one of the most serious moments in the recent history of Guatemala. First, because it has not been common in the Central American country for the business sector to oppose a presidential decision. Too many presidents have opted to follow the road marked by business owners without ever daring to deviate one inch from it.

Secondly, had the management boycott succeeded, Guatemala would have had to halt all investment in social development and infrastructure, which would have in turn provoked a sudden curb in the nation's growth. The political consequence of this scenario is easy to imagine: the triumph of the extremes. The guerrillas would have proved that there is no place for social development in government, and the country would have been forced to respond to the guerrilla challenge by increasing military activity. In other words, Guatemala would be now at the idle point it had been for decades, with the difference that the rest of its neighbors are making progress and are no longer engaged in civil wars.

Under the circumstances, President De León Carpio did what should be expected of a democratic leader. He went to Congress, exposed the gravity of the situation, and gained broad political support to confront the businessmen.

With the weight of the legislative branch behind him, and an extremely pertinent use of the Constitution, the President defeated the maneuver and the nation regained its revenues. This allowed the continuation of social investment, infrastructure development, and the struggle to overcome one of the most serious problems of the developing world — shortage of energy.

Without a doubt, De León Carpio's versatile skills permitted him to reach the presidency at a critical moment and has later guaranteed the solution to the crisis. It is not up to me to judge Ramiro de León Carpio's personality; I leave that to people who have a much closer relationship with him. I can assure, however, that, in general, societies remember under a gentler light those leaders who, like him, act with caution, without imposing his decisions, and consulting many people. This breed of statesmen, unfortunately, is not in abundance these days. But it will be totally within his character for President De León Carpio to transfer to his democratic successor a nation much more respectful of the Constitution than the one he found when he took office.

To move ahead on the road of dialogue and respect for the law sounds simple, but it amounts to the greatest revolution Guatemala has known in the present century. Ramiro de León Carpio is entitled to claim a major part of the success.

Santiago Aroca
Miami, July 1995

Appendix A

Impact of Tax Reform on Guatemalan Revenue Budget *(In millions of quetzals)*

Income Tax		
Increment of the income tax rate from 25% to 30% (including Q95 million from taxes on commercial and agricultural enterprises)	Q 308.00	
Revision of income tax rates for individuals based on paying ability	-9.00	
Tax on financial products	60.00	
Quarterly payment of income tax	210.00	
Payment of quota of commercial enterprises	50.00	
Increment of Income Tax		Q 619.00
Value Added Tax		
Increment of 3%	750.00	
Reforms on closing loopholes and reducing exemptions	100.00	
Increment of Value Added Tax		Q 850.00
Other Taxes		
Tax on vehicle circulation	40.00	
Tax on liquor	19.0	
Increment on Other Taxes		Q 59.00
Legislative-Administrative Measures		
Tax Crime and Creation of Tax Courts	150.00	150.00
Tax Increment on Taxable Income for 1996 as a Result of Existing Legislation		Q 1,678.00

Source: The President of Guatemala

Chronology

300 B.C.-900 A.D. — The Mayan civilization flourished in Guatemala during this period, according to most archaeologists. The Mayas created a highly developed society, as proven by the Tikal pyramids and the ruins of Uaxaclún and Piedras Negras. In the year 300 the Mayan calendar appeared.

900 — For reasons historians have not been able to determine, the Mayan society entered an era of decay as of this year. When the Spanish conquerors arrived, the Indians were not aware of the existence of the wheel, steel weapons, and the use of animals for transporting cargo.

987 — Toltecs invaded Yucatán.

1400-1475 — The Quichés occupied a great part of the highlands.

1519 — Hernán Cortes disembarked in Mexico.

1524 — Pedro de Alvarado, heading a small army, and with the collaboration of several thousand Aztecs and Tlaxcalans, defeated the last Mayan resistance and seized the central valleys of what today is Guatemala.

1543 — The capital of La Nueva España (Guatemala) was established in the city of Antigua.

1570 — Spain created Guatemala's General Headquarters with jurisdiction over Chiapas, Yucatán, Nicaragua and Costa Rica.

1676 — The National University of San Carlos was founded in Guatemala.

1773 — An earthquake destroyed Antigua, which was later rebuilt in a new location more to the west under the name of Guatemala City.

1776 — The present Guatemala City was founded.

1821 — With the dissolution of the Spanish empire in America, Guatemala proclaimed its independence but within Mexico.

1823 — The National Constitutional Assembly of Guatemala proclaimed Central America's independence from Mexico. The Central American Federation was born with Guatemala as its capital.

1830 — The Honduran liberal Francisco Morazán became the president of the Central American Federation.

1837 — Rafael Carrera launched a popular rebellion to become Guatemala's dictator.

1838 — The Central American Federation was dissolved.

1865 — Rafael Carrera died after holding absolute power for more than a quarter century.

1871 — After a liberal revolt, dictator Rufino Barrios took power. He expelled the Jesuits and tried to rebuild the Central American Federation by force.

1885 — Rufino Barrios died in combat. He left behind the nation's first banking system.

1898 — Manuel Estrada Cabrera reached power and ruled despotically.

1906 — The United Fruit Company established its first banana plantations.

1920 — A popular revolt toppled Estrada Cabrera after 22 years of absolute power.

1931 — Jorge Ubico y Castañeda became dictator.

1944 — A student rebellion overthrew Ubico. Juan José Arévalo, a professor with strong democratic convictions, was elected president. He became the second president in Guatemala's history to pass on the presidency to a democratically elected successor.

1951 — Jacobo Arbenz Guzmán, a leftist military officer, was elected president.

1952 — President Arbenz embarked in economic reforms that affected the interests of large U.S. companies, such as the United Fruit Company and the International Railroads of Central America.

1954 — A group of exiles, trained and supported by the U.S. Central Intelligence Agency, invaded Guatemala and toppled President Arbenz. Col. Carlos Castillo Armas became the new president.

1957 — Col. Castillo Armas was murdered. Miguel Ydígoras Fuentes succeeded him in the presidency.

1963 — A *coup d'etat* toppled Ydígoras.

1966 — In what international observers considered a clean election, Julio César Méndez Montenegro, a left-wing politician, was elected president.

1967 — Guatemalan writer Miguel Angel Asturias was awarded the Nobel Prize for Literature.

1970 — Leftist guerrillas extended their activity to broad areas of the countryside and established permanent bases in departments in the jungle and in areas close to the Mexican border.

1976 — En earthquake caused 22,000 deaths in Guatemala City.

1982 — Gen. Angel Aníbal Guevara was elected president, but another general, Efraín Ríos Montt, replaced him after a military *coup d'etat.*

1983 — In yet another coup, Ríos Montt was overthrown by Gen. Oscar Mejía Víctores.

1985 — Christian Democrat Vinicio Cerezo was elected president.

1987 — The first peace talks between the government and the guerrillas began in Madrid, Spain.

1991 — Jorge Serrano Elías was elected president.

1992 — Rigoberta Menchú received the Nobel Peace Prize for her struggle in defense of Latin American indigenous people.

1993 — The Guatemalan Congress discharged Serrano Elías after attempting a self-coup from the presidency. Congress elected Ramiro de León Carpio, the nation's Human Rights Commissioner, as the new president.

Index of Names